Rants & Retorts

Rants & Retorts

HOW BIGOTS GOT A MONOPOLY ON COMMENTING ABOUT NEWS ONLINE

Anita M. Samuels

ISBN: 1535566566
ISBN 13: 9781535566568
Library of Congress Control Number: 2016912567
CreateSpace Independent Publishing Platform
North Charleston, South Carolina
Cover art by Jeffrey Rosenkrantz, JR Design
Author photo by Nancy Lalanne, Lalanne Photography

*For my mother and father
and Mrs. Thomas,
my high school English teacher*

Acknowledgements

THANK YOU, ISMAY E. SAMUELS and the late Bernard P. Samuels, my parents, who raised me.

Enormous thanks to Sandye Wilson, the greatest coach in the world, who with patience, encouragement, and strongly worded "pep talks," shoved me headfirst over the finish line of this project.

Love and positivity to my sister-friend journalist Janine Coveney, who since my first day at Billboard magazine in Los Angeles has been a beacon of friendship. Her advice and reality checks throughout this process have helped me to retain some of my sanity.

Gracious thanks to sister-friend journalist and author Julia Chance, whose advice and suggestions helped to point me in the right direction.

Love and gratitude to my longtime friend and colleague Jared McCallister, who witnessed my very first "WTF" moments about racist comments and who endlessly listened to my constant babbling about them, even at times when I am sure that he would have preferred to talk about other things.

My humble thanks to graphic designer Jeffrey Rosenkrantz for "getting it" and creating a phenomenal cover almost at the speed of light.

Respect and consciousness to journalist "Media Assassin" Harry Allen, who first told me I should write a book about online comments and who sent me loads of reader responses that made my eyeballs want to permanently invert themselves.

Respect and love to my New York Times mentors, Howard University journalism professor Yanick Rice Lamb and journalist and editor Angela P. Dodson, who took time out of their busy schedules to read through the muck and mire of an idea that has forever changed my psyche. I am also forever grateful to them and others for earlier nurturing the potential of a shy young woman from Long Island who wanted to write.

Thank you, Carlton "Chuck D" Ridenhour, for taking the time to discuss your views about online commenting. Like the messages in your immortal songs "Don't Believe the Hype" and "Shut 'Em Down," the bottom line is always worth fighting for.

I must also thank family, friends, and colleagues, whether they listened to my constant and sometimes annoying contemplations about online racist rants, offered encouragement, or sent me comments to consider using. I also want to express my appreciation to all of the professionals who allowed themselves to be interviewed for this book, providing me with invaluable help in bringing "Rants & Retorts: How Bigots Got a Monopoly on Commenting About News Online" to fruition.

Thank you, Brooklyn Borough President Eric Adams, lawyers Norman Siegel, Adrian Solomon, Brett E. Lewis, Iyana Titus, and William Turner; Editorsoncall LLC, Ingrid Sturgis, New York City Councilwoman Laurie Cumbo, psychologists Brenda Wade, Janice Walters, and Monnica Williams; anthropologist Sabhiya Price, Denise Wheeless, Arjuna Routte-Prier, Albert Kimson, Shane Samuels, Franz Martin, Margaret Barrow, Andrew P. Smallwood, Karla Zelaya, Norine Smith, Tabitha Smith, Sarah Smith, Carlton Smith, Russell Samuels, Vernenci Samuels, Kayla Samuels, Keith Woods, E. Ethelbert Miller, Sync Studios Brooklyn, Robert S. Anthony, Havelock Nelson, Kellyn A. Tillers, Allison Samuels, David Sheddon, Walter Middlebrook, Edward Fay, The Poynter Institute, Ana Daniels, José Sierra, William M. Roane, the international media professionals networking group "Black Girls Rule: Absolutely Anything Goes," Tomika Anderson, Michael Days, Eugene Holley, Gary Caesar, Mary Curtis, Richard Prince, Lena Williams, Claudia Payne, Bob Butler, Wendi C. Thomas, Mark Potok, Keith Woods, Nichele Hoskins, Steve

Freeman, Omar Wasow, the late Dori Maynard, Gregory L. Moore, Tiffany James, Nathan Whyte, The Maynard Institute, Paul Greenberg, Morris Thompson, Frank Steele, Rukiya Goddard, Kate Hartley, Carrot Communications (London), Wendy Christie, Emoderation (London), Julie Gallagher, Sarah Hawk, Jen O'Driscoll, and Suvi Manneh.

Foreword

AUTHOR AND JOURNALIST ANITA SAMUELS first hit me up in March of 2013 in a "direct message" on Twitter about the book that she was writing about online racist comments against African-Americans. She wanted to know if I would participate in her project. I responded by saying that the topic was "deep" and that I wanted to be a part of it.

She and I first met in 1996 for "Back to the Terrordome," a story she wrote for The Source magazine about "The Autobiography of Mistachuck," my first solo album as the founder of the rap group Public Enemy. It turned out that we both were from Roosevelt, Long Island, and that she remembered my mother, who worked at Roosevelt Junior-Senior High School.

In this book, Anita describes how destructive online comments are being dealt with by news organizations and offers solutions to the problem. Although I can't recall the very first racist comment that I ever read on a news website, my first response was: "Don't you think that the fact that legitimate news sites provide comment areas, and that they are so liberal with the comment areas, is a mark against the news site as well? Because they allow that negativity just to be on there, instead of screening a person's comment and scraping it off? Letting an idiot speak is usually a bad thing."

The public outrage over racist and other negative and offensive comments, Anita says, have caused some online publications to use human and electronic moderators, others to limit comment options on specific stories, and still others to eliminate comments.

These are steps in the right direction but, like Anita, I think more should be done to stop the continuous flow of racist and sometimes threatening language. The way I see it, the writer and the editor of the original story might be responsible and respectable, but the commenters are horrible. If it was 1946 and somebody wrote a handwritten letter, of course with misspellings and everything with a backwards "r" saying "nigger go home," then that would be construed as a threat. Even if it is written through a computer system and an Internet service provider, isn't that also a threat?

Allowing online racist comments about African-Americans is like legitimizing that scrawled Nazi hate mail of "nigger die, nigger go home." It's as if 500,000 James Earl Rays (the white man convicted of assassinating the Rev. Dr. Martin Luther King Jr.) were out there reading news and writing comments every day. I know one thing: The Internet providers are the ones who should be held liable for allowing this racism to go through. People should be traced to their words. I think you would have a fraction of people saying that limiting these types of comments is encroaching upon their freedoms of speech and expression, but I'm saying hate mail is hate mail. Whether a person is in your face saying that they hate you and want to kill you, or whether a person does it online anonymously, it's still a threat to your well-being. So those people need to be addressed and dealt with.

People who write comments should not be able to say, "I'm going to kill you" or "I'm going to harm you," without it being traced. They have to be accountable for their words. Just because they say it behind a cloak, i.e. "You don't know who I am — you might never know who I am, but watch your ass," you have to take that seriously. At any other time, someone would track that down or do their best to track that down. This is what the American civil rights struggle had to go through in the 1960s. It wasn't so much about the in-your-face racism of the people that came out like a Bull Connor, the commissioner of public safety for the city of Birmingham, Alabama, who sicced police dogs and turned fire hoses on peaceful protesters. The people behind the Ku Klux Klan cloaks and masks and robes were the real danger to African-Americans.

Nobody really knew initially who set that bomb off in the 16th Street Baptist Church in Birmingham on Sept. 15, 1963, killing Addie Mae Collins, Denise McNair, Carole Robertson, and Cynthia Wesley. It just came from a whole bunch of people who were cowards, who hid themselves. Years later, three Klan members were individually tried and convicted in the case. In online comments, avatars and fake names have the tendency to be the new KKK hoods of the New Millennium.

News organizations and other websites must be accountable for what they allow on their sites. It should be as things are done in the radio industry. If a person curses on the radio, someone from the Federal Communications Commission will go and tell that station that they now have, say, a $17,000 fine. Each affiliate that is attached to the station will also be fined $17,000, so if you have 10 affiliates, it's a $170,000 fine that will shut people up. So if some comment-policing organization existed and it fined an ISP for unacceptable comments, that would clear that up very quickly. It's not as if there were a trillion of them, so they could be identified.

I think Anita's book is going to help make a change by identifying the people who seem to have the most at stake here, the service providers that allow anonymous comments. They may not know the identities of the people writing the comments, but those people have to pay a bill to keep their Internet on. People at the top of the pile [executives] have to be able to say: "We're accountable for all of this language that goes across the United States of America and beyond. We have to make sure that comments, at least in the realm of what we're dealing with here, are non-offensive."

Unfortunately, not all people in our society are normal and decent, so you can't have normal dialogue in online comments. Most people who are online probably never wrote a letter. People don't have time to sit down and write a letter. If you really liked something back in the day, you wrote a letter to say you loved it, and it probably never was read. Now, you have a platform that makes it really easy for somebody who is stupid — by that I mean uninformed, biased, angry — or someone who just enjoys sparking controversy to make outrageous comments.

I don't expect comments to go away, but I know that if they did, nobody would miss anything.

Carlton "Chuck D" Ridenhour, 2014
Founder, hip-hop group Public Enemy
Ventura, California

Table of Contents

Acknowledgements· vii

Foreword· ·xi

Preface · xvii

Chapter 1   The Freedom of Racist Speech · · · · · · · · · · · · · · · · · · · 1

Chapter 2   Fear of a Black President: 2008 Campaign, Election,
             and 2012 Reelection Aftermath· · · · · · · · · · · · · · · · · · · 36

Chapter 3   Altercations With Police · 57

Chapter 4   Black Women: Bad Choices? · · · · · · · · · · · · · · · · · · · 71

Chapter 5   Equal Education· 102

Chapter 6   Black Men and the Animal Instinct · · · · · · · · · · · · · · 114

Chapter 7   Mama's Little Babies · 143

Chapter 8   Please Report Offensive Posts!!!! · · · · · · · · · · · · · · · · 158

Index· 177

About the Author · 185

Preface

IN 2008, I BECAME PREOCCUPIED with the racist comments people make about articles published on the Internet. I had long ignored the comments sections on Web pages, but then I began to take notice of the ones I saw on NYDailynews.com because I read it regularly for local news and because I have been writing for it for many years. I dove in with an open mind, reading what turned out to be mostly negative comments, seemingly in response to any article in which the subject was identified as African-American. The writers did not use sugarcoated, pretty, or cutesy words. The comments were expressions of pure, unadulterated hatred, like this one posted by a NYDailynews.com reader:

> "I used to think blacks were just stupid, now I'm convinced that they're mentally unfit. Everytime they don't get their way, it's some great white plot against them. How about they just grow up!!!" – Posted by fortherecord111222, NYDailynews.com

(Note: The comments I have found are frequently misspelled and ungrammatical with sentences or thoughts that are incomplete. I cut and pasted them into the manuscript exactly as they appeared on the Internet. I use them throughout the book "as is," except to avoid the use of profane words. [The readers sometimes use symbols in place of profanity or other offensive words to get past the filters. I have

not changed symbols used in place of omitted letters.] Deletions from the original
may be indicated by an ellipsis [...].)

This comment, in response to "Keys' gangsta theory a load of rap?" April 14, 2008, was the very first comment that I complained about to an editor at the New York Daily News. It was eventually removed.

The story, about an interview published in Blender magazine in which Grammy-award winning singer Alicia Keys said that "gangsta rap," the hardcore subgenre of hip-hop music, was a "government ploy to convince black people to kill each other." Keys added that the government and the media perpetuated a fatal feud "to stop another great black leader from existing." The feud was between rappers Tupac Shakur, who was shot several times in a drive-by on Sept. 7, 1996, in Las Vegas, Nevada, and died from his wounds six days later, and Christopher Wallace, aka The Notorious B.I.G., who died in a drive-by shooting in Los Angeles, California, on March 9, 1997.

Keys' comments ignited controversy among readers, many of whom commented. The April 14 story quoted an online reader, "Nettie2ka," who said she hoped that Keys didn't make the comments. If she did, the reader said, "she is clearly the dumbest person on the planet."

While others thought Keys was brave to speak her mind, I was surprised that Keys would make such questionable comments, given her status in the music industry. However, I felt that the reader "fortherecord111222" had dropped an unexpected racist bomb into the fray. Plenty of white people have all kinds of conspiracy theories about the government, but they are not, as a race, deemed stupid and mentally unfit for espousing them.

It was then that I started reading comments more closely and attempting to have those I viewed as offensive to black people removed. I found, though, that I was simply unable to keep up with the sheer volume of them and that it would be impossible to control the level of racism that was being spewed on a daily basis.

At first, I would email the comments that I considered to be insulting to a New York Daily News editor and follow up with a call to complain.

That person would speak to someone else, and often the comment disappeared. This appeased me only for a short time. As I continued to read them, I developed what I called "comment whiplash." Each time I read one, my head and neck would jerk backward, as if I were slamming on the brakes of a car.

On Nov. 25, 2006, Sean Bell, a young black bridegroom, was killed by cops who fired 50 bullets at the car he was in outside a Queens strip club after his bachelor party on the morning he was to wed his fiancée. In 2008, during the trial of the three cops who were accused of killing Bell, attorneys were often quoted in news reports about how they thought the trial would end. In "Top Defense Lawyers: Cops will beat the rap in Sean Bell Case," published in the New York Daily News on April 16, 2008, attorneys were quoted as saying the three accused officers would be acquitted.

Most readers weren't too surprised when that verdict was announced on April 25, 2008. In the midst of a very emotional and divided conversation online about the article came this:

"…Well since everyone says I am a racist anyway - I'll give you something you can all eat up. It kicks a$$ to be white! Comedian Chris Rock said it best… and I quote "There is a white, one-legged bus boy who won't trade places with my black a$$…and I'm rich. That's how good it is to be white." He is a very smart man, and his statement is very true. I understand your bitterness: people hate you, the cops profile you and some in your community give you all a bad name. If that were me, I'd be bitter too. I wake up every morning with a world of opportunity and I take advantage of it. I wouldn't trade place with any of you. I'm white and of western European background. The cops treat me like I am gold, I can do illegal things and get away with it because of my innocent looking face- no one ever suspects the white girl. It is good to be white… call me what you will, throw all the insults you want, but I will wake up tomorrow and still be a happy white person… and that makes your blood boil" – Posted by cunard, NYDailynews.com

The readers of NYDailyNews.com do not have a monopoly on this sort of off-the-wall racist verbiage. I live in New York City where I read a variety of websites for local news, and other sites reflected this phenomenon as well.

In May 2008, comments on a Newsday.com story caught my eye. It was about administrators for the Roosevelt Union Free School District on Long Island calling for a 3 percent tax hike to cover the upcoming year's budget. So did another story later published about the district having a $9 million surplus, allowing it to propose significant spending for student services.

Because I had lived in Roosevelt from the time I was 3 years old into my early teen years, and it did not always have a good reputation, my interest was piqued.

The story apparently struck a chord with online commenters, too. Some complained that blacks were lazy, ignorant and groomed to take handouts.

One said: "Cut back on the watermelons at lunch." Naively, I attempted to understand what watermelons had to do with a tax hike. While this was clearly meant as a joke, it also made me realize how problematic comments were going to become. When I began to talk to friends about what I saw as a trend toward uncivilized, blatantly racist speech, they expressed mixed reactions. Some solemnly agreed that the online comments were ruthless, while others shrugged it off, suggesting that today's racism was no different from what African-Americans experienced years, decades, and centuries ago. Still more suggested that perhaps this trend reflected reality because some African-Americans were doing things that fed into stereotypes.

Eventually, several close friends — the ones who had listened to my constant complaints — told me that I was onto something. They said that if I was this passionate about the racist comments, I should consider writing a book. In the end, I decided that the commentary should be documented as a 20th-century tool for the high-speed spread of racism by laypeople — not always obvious white supremacists. Perhaps it is the person who was working on a laptop at Starbucks, using a computer at a library, or sitting at an office cubicle next to any one of us as they post their racist views under assumed names.

I remembered that my motivation for becoming a journalist in the early 1990s was to help ensure that people of all races could read more positive stories about black people. In fact, I wrote many of the stories that I have done in the last 23 years with the hope of inspiring people. The groundswell of negative commentary about African-Americans seemed to cancel out any contribution I had made to my race. I thought that maybe my friends were right — that I was being too sensitive, too thin-skinned or taking it too personally. How could I not with comments such as this reaction to the tax-hike story suggesting that blacks seemed to be a "burden" on taxpayers?

"It costs a fortune for White Society to maintain **** Population because Blacks can't do it themselves. Name one thriving harmonious Black Country in all of Africa. Or one thriving Black Community in the World for that matter. Bet you can't. That might sound Racist but it's a fact and it's the truth so I could care less what some Liberal thinks about my statement." – Posted by Lib Hater, West Islip, N.Y., Newsday.com

I thought that if this was the general perception of my race, then we would never be seen as anything but stereotypes now and forever. To me, it did not matter that some of the stories that drew racist comments were about African-Americans who had done bad things. Plenty of people of other races commit the same crimes, including murders, burglaries, or cop killings. White people face the same issues that we do — everything from teen pregnancies, sexual violence, and single parenthood to poor judgments in relationships. Nonetheless, I was seeing literally in black and white that a double standard existed for African-Americans.

I began to get very irritated about what I was reading and concerned about the effect that it would have on African-Americans as a whole. I even wondered how long these types of comments would remain in Internet archives, on the off chance that some African-American elementary student researching a book report in the distant future might stumble upon the vile words. I imagined how any child would feel reading hateful words about any black person that they admired, including President Barack Obama. The child or adult might shrug it off and go back to playing video games or chatting with their friends on Facebook or Meebo, but it could affect them for much longer than anyone ever imagined.

As we have learned over the years, anything posted on the Web could stay out there indefinitely. An administrator might remove something offensive from a publication's official site under pressure, but since it was already released into cyberspace, millions of people probably have read it and been negatively affected by it, and the articles and comments could remain stored or cached somewhere. With the advent of social media, it also could have been retweeted, pinned, shared, or liked by millions more people.

In April 2008, I began collecting racist Internet comments with a greater intensity. Every day without fail, I compiled comments from as many websites as I could. I found the same trend toward nasty, racist commentary.

On the Miami Herald website on May 7, 2008, for instance, "seawolf" wrote this in response to an article about a murder and an alleged suspect in police custody:

"NI66ER SHOOTS NI66ER, SO WHAT ELSE IS NEW? NI66ER SHOOTS CHINAMAN, NI66ER SHOOTS WHITE MAN, NI66ER SHOOTS HIS DOG. NI66ER ROBS STORE, NI66ER ROBS BANK, NI66ER RUNS FROM COPS, NI66ER JACKS CAR."

I was frustrated because I could not understand how the companies who ran the websites could allow such racist postings to appear on them. I read the comments with breakfast in the mornings, day and night, and on weekends. The first six months were brutal. My eyes glazed over from the filth. Not unlike those posting whose names I began to recognize, I became addicted to reading the articles where race was a factor and the comments they inevitably drew. By 2010, I had collected hundreds of comments. I categorized them by topics: politics, education, parenting, relationships, and others.

As I catalogued my collection, I noticed that African-Americans had also begun to fight back against this brand of online racism by posting facts and corrections to counter the tirades. I found that these efforts still did not take the sting out of racist postings. It was very much like trying to cover a fatal, gaping wound with a Band-Aid. I knew that I would have to seek out background from organizations such as the Poynter Institute for Media Studies, a nonprofit school for journalism in St. Petersburg, Florida, and other media specialists in order to learn how racist Internet comments had prevailed in the manner that they had.

As it turned out, readers and editorial staff have made numerous complaints. Editors had to defend the practice of allowing comments on articles because of readers who were taking "free expression" to such sleazy levels.

From 2008 to 2011, a growing number of newspaper editors began monitoring comments more closely, frequently eliminating those they deemed offensive. Some organizations stopped allowing comments after a time, or simply eliminated the option for readers to comment when they published specific stories that would cause obvious racial backlash.

Ultimately, editors tried out a flurry of ideas to handle negative comments and the problems that they were creating. Among them were mandatory reader registrations, fancy comment rating systems, pay walls, automatic word filters, user bans, specialized user status, and public views showing that certain off-topic comments had been deleted. Those changes, though laudable, have not been enough. Online racist commentary is still pervasive.

In 2010, I stopped working for a while on what eventually became "Rants & Retorts: How Bigots Got a Monopoly on Commenting About

News Online." I had become depressed over the words that I had been reading every day for more than three years. No matter how much I tried, I couldn't get the racist comments out of my mind, and I didn't like the way they made me feel. It is terrible when anger gives way to feelings of hopelessness from written words of hate, and no matter what anyone says, these comments can affect one's self-esteem. I came back to the book in 2013, because I decided that the documentation of online racist comments is just as important as the Works Progress Administration's oral slave narratives in the 1930s. The online comments could serve as a written history of how some elements of society saw African-Americans in the 21st century.

The unedited comments that you will read within the pages of this book have invaded my thoughts, my dreams, and my life like an incurable virus. I am now convinced that regardless of African-Americans' accomplishments, even life-saving or world-changing feats, nothing will exterminate racist views and expressions of them against us. This experience of immersing myself in racist words will never leave me. I tend to keep my anger about it beneath the surface. If anything, it has been replaced by numbness. I thought I might stop reading comments at some point, but the addiction to do so sometimes takes over. I am less shocked at anything that I read now.

As a proud black woman, I'm still offended by racist comments, but I prefer to focus on the positive aspects of my race and continue to relish the countless accomplishments of African-Americans. As internationally acclaimed poet Anne Waldman often says: "Don't lament. Do something about it." This book, written proof that post-racial is a meaningless phrase, is what I'm doing about it.

Anita M. Samuels
Brooklyn

CHAPTER 1

The Freedom of Racist Speech

"Should we feel guilty for being so awesome and technological-ly advanced while Africans were dancing around fires like sav-age pagans? Its funny how you dont see Jesse Jackson or African Americans fighting for the rights of the many white women sold in sexual slavery around the world. Slavery still exists in africa google it. Africans enslave other Africans all the time sometimes its even a part of their religions. So white people stop feeling guilty and stop letting these people act like we were the only ones involved in it. In fact I think we should reconsider slavery for some of the people living on welfare for decades." – Posted by Pat21401, news. aol.com, May 25, 2009

USING THE INTERNET HAS BECOME the easiest way for us to exercise what we think is our First Amendment right to freedom of speech. Online sites — including the Web pages of such venerable news organizations as The New York Times and The Washington Post, and social media like Twitter, Facebook, and YouTube — have become readily accessible, in-ternational soapboxes where posting hateful views has become the norm. Online forums generate thousands upon thousands of racist comments every single day. More often than not, stories that directly or indirectly involve race attract this kind of ugly, racist, and degrading response.

Bob Butler, then president of the National Association of Black Journalists (2013-2015), the organization for African-American journalists, students, and media professionals established in 1975, does not think racist comments should be ignored.

"I think as African-Americans, we know that this is not a post-racial society," he said. "I think that people who are not of color need to see this to understand what we're saying. Some of these folks will think that everything's fine now, that racism doesn't exist. All you have to do is read these online comments, these comments, after a news story on a newspaper site and online websites to realize that we do still have racism in this country."

Those who post hateful comments tend to defend their rights to "free speech" vigorously, even if it means hurting others, but that reflects ignorance of what freedom of speech really means in terms of our constitutional rights.

Norman Siegel, a partner in the law firm Siegel Teitelbaum & Evans, LLP, specializes in freedom of speech issues. Freedom of speech and freedom of expression are not the same thing, he said.

"The concept of freedom of speech is always in the context of the First Amendment vis-à-vis government. I always have to remind people that the First Amendment only applies to government action, so if you have expression in the private sector, you can't say free speech; you have to talk about free expression," he explained. "Expression is broader than just free speech; that's an important fact. I think that most people think that they support free speech/free expression. The real test is: Do you support it when the content of the speech is something you disagree with? Very often people don't support the right of the person who says something they don't agree with."

Robert S. Anthony, a syndicated computer columnist who also writes the blog "The Paper PC," said, "Sometimes the give and take on blogs, news sites, and elsewhere on the Internet is fairly tame and reasonable."

For most, access to the "information superhighway" through online services began in the late 1980s or 1990s.

Most users of the Internet were white, male, and middle-aged, and the online commentary reflected that. "This is no longer the case, of course,"

Anthony said. "Today anti-black comments are often quickly challenged by other comments. While the Internet can be anonymous, it's also transparent, and most of today's users seem savvy enough to see through hateful messages."

Because racism is opinion-based, it is hard to erase negativity that has stereotyped African-Americans for decades, and demands for "free speech" allow it to continue.

Janice Walters, a psychology professor at the Borough of Manhattan Community College who is originally from Australia, has worked extensively with Aborigines, and her students in Manhattan are primarily African-American.

"I think free speech is great, but not when it's at the detriment of another person," she said. "I mean, we have to be respectful of other people. If free speech is an attack or an assault on someone else, either an individual or a whole race, it is not OK. There are limits. There is a way to express what you want to."

Walters also said that a person's perception of other races is what makes them treat people a certain way. "Whether it's racist comments or otherwise, all you're doing is putting everyone in one group and saying, 'You all fit this category' or for example, 'You're all bad people,' because that's your perception. Your perception is pretty distorted."

There were early signs that the Internet could be troublesome. The first attempt to regulate it came in the form of Section 230 of the Communications Decency Act, also known as Title V of the Telecommunications Act of 1996, signed into law by President Bill Clinton. The intention was to make it a criminal offense to transmit knowingly "patently offensive, indecent, and obscene materials" to children under 18 years of age.

On Feb. 8, 1996, free-speech advocates filed a lawsuit opposing what they considered to be proposed restrictions that would affect regular adult usage of the Internet, in violation of the U.S. Constitution's guarantee of free speech. In June 1997, the U.S. Supreme Court agreed and eliminated those provisions, but not without inadvertently benefiting Internet providers. Ultimately, Section 230 made Internet providers (ISPs) immune, protecting them and users from any liability for material posted on their websites by a third party; i.e., the reader.

While those fights dealt with content that might be pornographic or obscene, the topic of negative commentary online did not enter the public discourse again until 2001, possibly after 9/11, when, said David Shedden, director of the Poynter Institute's Eugene Patterson Library, online newspapers began allowing the public to vent feelings about the disaster. Shedden maintains the institute's "New Media Timeline" about the history of new media and online journalism.

"Although the technology for user comments with individual articles has only developed during the past ten years, the history of readers commenting on stories with online chat rooms and discussion lists can likely be traced to the middle of the 1990s, and perhaps even earlier," Shedden said.

No one seems to know exactly when the comment forums as we know them today seem to have started.

"I have followed online community functions and the news for many years, but not closely enough to recall when I first saw message boards attached to the articles," said Internet analyst Omar Wasow in an interview for this book in 2014.

According to a New York Times article, "No Comments," on Sept. 20, 2013, early Internet comments were generated through the Bulletin Board System, or BBS, which was accessed by dial-in modem, allowing users to — among many other functions — exchange messages with others through email, message boards, and chat rooms.

"The computer code that determined the order in which text appears on a BBS also provides the early construction of the comment thread," the article said. From there, commenting functions evolved to include the "guestbook," where visitors could type in messages on websites, and "MoveableType," a publishing and blogging software developed by Six Apart in 2001.

Wasow, the co-founder and strategic advisor for BlackPlanet.com, a social networking website that targets African-Americans and launched in 1999, thinks there wasn't any one technological "breakthrough" that allowed news organizations to offer comment options to their readers.

"The Web was originally designed to be a publishing medium without a social component," Wasow said. "From the beginning, though, people have been hacking it to add social elements. Unfortunately, I don't have any insight as to when or what was critical to those tools being adopted by newspapers."

Discernible racist online postings against African-Americans likely began in the late 1990s, but in 2005, one instance that thrust the topic into the public eye was when James Wright of the Washington Afro-American newspaper wrote, "Black Fraternity's Move Spawns Racist Internet Messages," a Dec. 16, 2005, story about how the Zeta Zeta Chapter of Omega Psi Phi Fraternity, one of the oldest black Greek-letter fraternities, became the target of racist postings on fratty.net, a national fraternity/sorority website. According to Wright, the black fraternity's plan to build a house in the all-white Greek village of the University of South Carolina, where white fraternities and sororities own many mansions, had sparked the following insults:

"I propose throwing a cotton picking party for them when they move in. a thousand pounds of cotton in the front yard. Sure jesse jackson will be here in a heart beat, but it will be funny as hell watching them pick it up." – Re:USC Greekvillage/Reply No. 2 on Oct.24, 6:38pm via fratty.net

"That cotton idea is funny as ****and a great way to set the tone for their time here. Hopefully, the house never actually gets built, though. It will only bring loud niggers, even louder n*****b*****, and trashy ***wiggers and white-trash girls around. But hopefully Darwin was right these spooks will wind up tearing the house down in a week or two. Much longer than that and we'll have to do it for them. What do you say guys? Heres to ridding the village of our african-american infestation." – Re:USC Greekviollage/Reply No. 8 on October 25, 1:02 a.m. via fratty.net

Those anonymous comments caused USC to reexamine the racial climate on their campus. University officials did contact the national Greek organizations of students whom it could identify by their postings to the website. A direct result was that Kappa Sigma fraternity kicked out a white student for racist comments that he posted to the fratty.net website. Other members of Kappa Sigma were required to undergo racial-sensitivity training. The fratty.net website was deleted in 2006, reportedly over "Terms of Service" violations, but it is not known if the Kappa Sigma racist comment incident was the root cause of its demise.

In today's world, comment threads with racism specifically targeting African-Americans could easily be mistaken for a boxing match where opponents use words to jab the opponent with statements like these taken from online sites:

- "Black people think they're entitled to handouts."
- "Black girls just lay around, breed and collect welfare and food stamps."
- "Black men are all criminals who want to rape white women."
- "Black children are stupid."
- "Black people are useless."

More often than not, racist language in comments against blacks habitually seems aimed at dehumanizing the entire race, rather than targeting the individual or individuals under discussion in the article. Often, the racist observations are not even relevant to the topic at hand.

One absurdity that sticks out in the world of online commenting is that the remarks are more often than not riddled with grammatical errors, typos, and misspellings. I would think it should also be embarrassing to the news organization that allowed them to appear unedited.

Perhaps errors are rampant because so many people write many negative comments in haste and anger, as if to spew the hateful words as quickly as they can. Pressing "ENTER" to publish for some commenters must be like flushing a toilet, or maybe projectile vomiting.

"That goes back to how are people being educated," said Michael Days, editor of the Philadelphia Daily News, who is African-American. "Are they being educated? Some of that is just a thing that deals with schools and our standards. I grew up in the '50s and '60s, and we all had our language, our teenage language we used, but we knew how to switch. I guess what scares me now is that a lot of people do not know what formal English is. It's really just terrible."

Gregory L. Moore, former editor of The Denver Post (2002-2016), also African-American, thinks comments with grammatical errors are embarrassing.

"You jump to conclusions, we all do, about the person being ignorant and stuff because they can't write a simple grammatical sentence," he said. "That's something we should care about as a society. Not only is the level of discourse coarse and vulgar, but the whole skill of writing is disappearing as well. It's scary."

Whether they are written in the "standard English" or in "text-speech," technology's abbreviated and lazy way of writing, many comments still get their racist viewpoints out to the masses.

To be clear, it appears that two types of people post racist comments online:

* So-called "regular folks" who would never speak in public about their real views about minorities.
* White supremacists who "double dip" by going on known hate websites and to news websites.

The hate sites include Stormfront.org, founded by former Alabama Ku Klux Klan Grand Dragon Don Black and said to be one of the first forums to appear on the Internet in 1995, and Vanguard News Network (VNN), launched in 2000 by white nationalist Alex Linder.

"If you go on one of these hate forums, people are cheering each other on, and they are actually having discussions about individuals and trends within their worlds. Their written comments do not have the same pugnacious tone," said Mark Potok, editor-in-chief of the Southern Poverty Law Center (SPLC) publication "Intelligence Report," "Hatewatch" blog, and the Alabama-based organization's investigative reports. He was interviewed for this book in 2014.

"When you go to news sites in the comments sections, I think you see a lot more belligerence," Potok said. "It's rather different. You'll see people getting into extended arguments and 'flame wars', basically. You don't see discussions of the internal dynamics of the [hate] movement on news websites. There would be no purpose. They [white supremacists] are writing to people who already agree with them."

Potok is an award-winning journalist who covered many stories, including the 1993 Waco siege during a raid by Texas law enforcement at the compound of the Branch Davidians, a religious sect that broke from the Davidian Seventh-day Adventists. That raid resulted in the deaths of more than 80 people when the building caught fire. He also covered the 1995 Oklahoma City bombing that killed 168 people and the trial of the culprit, American terrorist Timothy McVeigh.

Potok told me that statements on a news website from a white supremacist will likely be something like: "This is how black people are," "This is the way Jews are," or "90 percent of the crime in America is committed by African-Americans."

"I think there are many people who post on white supremacist forums and then go on and make a whole bunch of comments on news sites," Potok said. "But I don't think — and this is my own opinion, and I have no way of verifying this — I don't think that the bulk of racist comments on mainstream sites come from professional racists … people from this sort of hate-group world. I think the vast majority come from more or less everyday people hiding behind the anonymity of the Internet."

When the culprit of a crime is identified as African-American, commenters seem to feel justified in using statistics that they have read or been told about, flawed and otherwise, to support their hatred. In response to the Sept. 19, 2008, Chicago Tribune piece "Boys, 14, 15, face life in prison" about two cousins who beat a Kenosha, Wisconsin, woman to death with a baseball bat to steal an Xbox gaming console, some readers who commented felt comfortable with the "facts" as they knew them:

> "Blacks may not like the statistics but they are what they are. All colors of people commit crimes but not to the same degree. It seems like Blacks are in the news all the time for something - crime or complaining." – Posted by BillCosby, ChicagoTribune.com

Keith Woods, vice president for diversity in news and operations at National Public Radio in Washington, D.C., and dean of faculty at the Poynter Institute in St. Petersburg, Florida, from 2005 to 2009, has followed the trend.

"The Internet makes it possible to spread all manner of vile ideas about all groups — just as it's made it possible to learn the most obscure facts in a matter of seconds," he said. "What the Internet provides is 'cover.' People can instantly post anonymously (or using pseudonyms) without having to face consequences. They could always do that with phone calls or mail, but they can do it with virtually no hassle now."

Woods also points out that the Internet also provides what he calls an "unfettered freeway between thought and action."

"For the people who might be inclined to think twice about expressing their more objectionable expressions, the Internet removes the moderating hand of time and replaces it with instant gratification," he said.

"I find that the bigotry makes me less likely to read the comments at the ends of stories, and I have little tolerance for the stupidity often found in blogs," Woods said.

Norman Siegel, who from 1985 to 2000 served as director of the New York Civil Liberties Union (NYCLU), a leading civil rights organization, thinks online comments are "horrible," but doesn't see things changing for the better.

"When I read that stuff, it turns my stomach. But then it gives a dose of reality, that you don't get taken away and thinking you're in la-la land, when we really still have these problems, so you have to re-educate yourself to the position of equal justice under the law," Siegel said. "Without that, you might get lulled into a false sense of security and complacency in thinking that the dream has been fulfilled. My position is that I want people to say what's on their minds, and I don't want any barriers, restrictions or chills in the air to hold back people expressing their inner thoughts, even if their inner thoughts are repugnant, hostile, racist, sexist, homophobic, whatever."

After spending time in the South in the 1960s as a young law student observing and witnessing the racial hostility there, Siegel believes that it's more dangerous for people to hide their thoughts. Allowing them to post online, he thinks, provides the opportunity to confront racism openly.

Paul Greenberg, the program director of the Media Arts and Journalism Department at Tulane University in New Orleans, said he also believes online commenting should be unrestricted.

In an interview for this book in 2015, he said: "I think that comments online should be wide open for anyone and everyone who has anything to say, because I believe that everybody's voice is as important as anyone else's voice. I feel very, very strongly about that."

Although online comments are what he and others consider to be "citizen journalism," he told me that commenting is communication and that he did not understand the need to control communication.

The Anti-Defamation League (ADL), an organization whose mission is "to stop the defamation of the Jewish people, to secure justice and fair treatment to all citizens," also takes the position that even the worst opinions, whether they appear in print or online, are protected under the First Amendment.

The Frequently Asked Questions section on ADL's website includes "Responding to Extremist Speech Online." It says, "Blanket statements expressing hatred of an ethnic, racial, or religious nature are protected by the First Amendment, even if those statements mention individual people and even if they cause distress in those individuals."

Steve Freeman, director of civil rights for the New York chapter of the organization, said that it has been looking at various forms of online hate speech since the early days of Web-based bulletin boards. "It's the dark side of the Internet, but it's always been there," he said. "Each new format or each new platform that comes out, that's a part of it, unfortunately."

Although the ADL does receive complaints about negative comments, representatives rarely speak out on someone's behalf. They usually tell whoever is complaining to see if the comment can be "flagged" for the publication that it appears under, Freeman said.

"Usually, although not always, those comments are moderated in some way, and if there's a flagging mechanism and somebody complains, then the company or the news source, whoever it is, will look at it and decide if it violates their terms of service, and they will take it down if it does," he said.

If that still doesn't work, Freeman adds, ADL might, on a case-by-case basis, say something about the comments, but only if ADL shares the view that they are offensive. Even if that happens, any responses from the ADL would be based on a pattern of racist commenting (anti-Semitism, anti-black, anti-Christian, etc.), rather than one particular comment.

On some levels, Butler of NABJ, who is also a news reporter for KCBS Radio in San Francisco, California, agrees with Siegel, the free-speech attorney, about letting people have their say. He isn't sure that comment moderation, something that is supposed to help minimize negative responses, is the solution to the rampant racism on news sites.

"I would say that you can't monitor everything," he said. "I mean, if they're going hire people just to monitor sites, do you want to censor people's comments like that? Wouldn't you want people to be who they really are? I almost think that it's better to let these comments be published so that people understand that there's a serious issue. I don't know if it's right to censor them."

Other media watchers have weighed in on the problem in print. In the June 12, 2008, article "Hate Speech Infests Online Versions of Local Daily Newspaper," published in the Pasadena Weekly, Deborah Lauter, director of the national civil rights division of the Anti-Defamation League, sounded a clear alarm against negative comments on the Internet, saying, "It's democracy gone wild."

A Monterey County Herald editorial, "Courts could restore civility to Web forums," published Sept. 20, 2009, said, "There was once hope that the interactive aspect of the Internet would be used to enrich the public dialogue, especially through the use of Web sites run by newspapers and other news outlets." Instead, the piece said, the newspaper industry had made a bit of a mess with it, resulting in written "slugfests" involving mostly anonymous participants, many of whom viewed online forums as arenas for "vituperation," rather than enlightenment.

The notion of "kumbaya" moments happening in the discussions online was over.

However, as Woods at NPR said, the Internet did not "create" the negativity that appears in comments sections. "The vile ideas were already there long before Google," he said.

In 2001, the U.S. Congress passed the No Child Left Behind Act, a law that required states to establish assessments for all students at select grade levels in order to receive federal funds. The purpose of the act was to track academic progress and improve outcomes for "disadvantaged" black and Hispanic children. This resulted in a flurry of stories about how well those efforts worked. A New York Times article, "No Child' Law Is Not Closing a Racial Gap," on April 28, 2009, said that from 2004 to 2009, "scores for young minority students increased, but so did those of white students, leaving the achievement gap stubbornly wide. …"

Some Times readers, presumably upscale, educated people, used the comments section to condemn black students with responses like this:

"...We need to say that which shall not be spoken. By the third grade, the natural course of black school children permanently reflects intellectual inferiority to whites, Asians, and Latinos (language adjusted) in learning skills development and ability..." – Posted by acting white dot com, Oakland, CA- NYTimes.com

Based on the name of the poster, "actingwhite dot com," it likely was an Internet troll looking to incite racial tension. The name refers to a disputed theory some educators have espoused that black children don't try to excel academically because they fear that peers will think of them as "acting white" or selling out.

Other readers suggested that perhaps the topic "No Child Left Behind" wouldn't be a big deal if white kids would stop doing "so well," and asked why Asians were not considered to be a "minority" in the piece. The takeaway comment from "Scott, CA," however, was that in the inner-city schools of Oakland and San Francisco, the cause of African-American academic deficits was the black community's "avoidance and denigration of academic achievement" in comparison with Asian kids, whose poor immigrant parents did not speak English and who attended the same schools as blacks and Hispanics. Those Asian students had amazingly "thrived and succeeded while the black kids usually fail," he said. He ended his diatribe with the admonition that "until there is a change in the black community, this cycle of failure will continue."

In an Oct. 31, 2007, radio broadcast of "All Things Considered," Tim Post of Minnesota Public Radio discussed how editors for the St. Cloud Times website were struggling with negative comments posted there. Post wrote: "It's the hot-button issues like politics, abortion, and crime that really fire people up in 'Story Chat.' But when the site carries a story that has anything to do with race, the comments pour in even faster, resulting in hundreds of postings in a few hours. Visitors, who aren't required to offer their real names on screen, often trade messages littered with racial stereotypes. Some worry those comments make the community look bad."

A story on the website about racial profiling, the controversial practice of law enforcement targeting race or ethnicity for suspected criminal activity, received more than 800 comments that included responses such as this:

> "What B.S. If they don't like it here I hope they don't let the door hit them on the butt on their way out. We all have had things about different departments that we felt were unfair. The difference is, we are white and adults so we realize that things happen and we can't let it color our life and sit around crying about it. I have seen so many things about blacks and somalians that I have disliked, but I don't dislike all blacks or somalians or Hispanics because of some. But I won't kiss their butts either to make them feel loved. There will always be divides in life, men /women..rich/poor..short/tall..good/bad ...intelligent/stupid...and you can't make all things equal. Grow up and get on with your life you sniveling idiots!" – Posted by chattycathy from Sartell-sctimes.com

Comments like the ones that appear in this book are mostly written under anonymous names. In the beginning, websites did not yet require one to sign in using a real name to be eligible to comment, as some websites require today.

Anonymity quickly became a problem. In one case that was not racial, the Gannett-owned paper Wausau Daily Herald, with a circulation of 21,000, named Dean Zuleger, a small-town politician, as its "Person of the Year," an honor that some members of the community apparently did not think he deserved.

Some readers wrote negative things about Zuleger's weight, salary, and management style. The local politician, who is white, took offense to nasty comments about him and demanded to know the source of what he deemed personal attacks. The paper, without a court order, gave Zuleger the then-anonymous commenter's email address. He turned out to be Paul Klocko, a businessman. Zuleger sent the man a letter on official stationery to stop saying the negative things and essentially to stop hiding behind the computer and meet him in person. But the paper admitted to making a mistake in exposing negative commenters.

Gannett Co. said at the time that its clarification about policies on anonymous speech was that it would now release information only if ordered by a court or if a comment contains a "threat of imminent harm."

David Ardia, director of the Citizen Media Law Project at Harvard Law School, was interviewed for the article "Wisconsin Paper Faces Backlash for Outing Web Critic," published by the Associated Press on Sept. 17, 2009, about the Zuleger case. "We're seeing a flood of cases involving anonymous comments," he said.

At the time, Ardia said: "If the community doesn't believe the paper has their back, then that's going to have a chilling effect on the kinds of speech people engage in on the paper's website."

While posters may believe that they have complete anonymity, law enforcement officials can expose their identities. In a few instances, readers who wrote offending words against specific people have faced legal challenges. They were "unmasked" by their Internet providers by court order for individuals who were suing the person.

The reality is that these cases go to court only if the comments include threats of "imminent" harm. However, it takes a long time to try such matters in court, if a complaint makes it that far, and involvement by a judge — even with a court order — may not always guarantee identification to victims of offensive comments.

In 2009, Richard Ottinger, a former New York congressman, did learn the name of the person who accused him in an online comment of corruption during a home renovation. However, when he brought a $1.5 million defamation suit against the individual (Ottinger v. Tiekert), it was thrown out of court because of the Strategic Lawsuits Against Public Participation, or anti-SLAPP, law. It states that in New York, individuals are sheltered from strategic lawsuits against "public participation."

It seems that the few individuals who have gotten court orders for the purpose of naming online commenters are politicians and others whose high-level status affords them the privilege of doing so. The average person would probably not be as successful.

Wendi C. Thomas, former Metro columnist for the Commercial Appeal in Memphis, Tennessee, wishes that comments would just go away. Thomas was the first black woman to hold the columnist title at the paper and a member of the Trotter Group, a national association of black columnists. She was reassigned from the position in June 2014 after 10 years as a columnist, and resigned from the paper soon after.

While at the paper, she said negative comments sometimes had a chilling effect on what she chose to write about.

"The comment boards of this newspaper are a toilet," she said. "I warn people that I write about not to read them. I've even not written stories because I didn't want to expose a subject to the online trolls. It's horrible, absolutely horrible."

Among her many negative experiences with racist comments was one that said she should be "locked in a storage shed" and another that said, "Folks like you should be lynched."

In her Aug. 2, 2012, column, "Subpoena targets bigoted bile," she quoted reader "Bartletteer." The reader had responded to reports that George Zimmerman, the former Florida neighborhood-watch volunteer later acquitted in the shooting death of the unarmed teenager Trayvon Martin, apologized to Martin's family at an April 20, 2012, bail hearing.

Thomas quoted Bartletteer as saying: "Zimmerman owes Thugvon's family nothing. No apology, nothing. They raised their sweet little boy to be a thug and predator and he got what he deserved. Thugvon was trash and so are his parents."

In her piece, Thomas discussed how the Shelby County Commission was criticized for naming her column, along with other articles by her and her colleagues, in a subpoena to learn the identities of commenters. They needed to prove that decision makers were influenced by bigoted constituents who made racist comments on the Appeal's website when they voted to keep their mostly white suburbs from having to unite with a mostly black Memphis school system in a unified district.

In the end, Thomas said the paper never turned over any information and the commission may have even withdrawn the motion. Days later, Thomas received what she called a "repentant" email from "Bartletteer" on Aug. 4, 2012:

Dear Ms. Thomas:

I am the online commenter Bartletteer. I can tell you I was shocked to see my screenname in the paper. I immediately cancelled my online account and won't be returning.

Since then I have done some soul searching and have reread some of my old posts and I didn't like the person I saw. I'm going to try very hard to be a better person in the future.

I want to thank you for helping me to look at myself in the mirror and acknowledge some very nasty aspects of myself.

I wish you well.

Sincerely,

D.W.

Although he sounded sincere, D.W./"Bartletteer" still got away with using only his initials without ever revealing his true name. He is also a coward for not publicly disclosing his alleged remorse in the very same public forum that allowed him to vent his racist views.

According to "Race Relations on Campus," a report published in 2006 in the Journal of Black Higher Education, just one white student from the Kappa Sigma fraternity at the University of South Carolina was kicked out of the brotherhood when it was revealed that he was one of several students who posted racist comments on the website fratty.net. Other anonymous offenders could not be identified.

The JBHE report is a national record of racial incidents that took place at the nation's institutions of higher learning. The Associated Press originally published it on Nov. 10, 2005.

African-American officers from the Philadelphia Police Department who filed a lawsuit against their employer and a white sergeant who allegedly spearheaded a racist website succeeded in having the site shut down. That did not erase the emotional toll it took on them.

David Greene, an attorney for the Electronic Frontier Foundation in San Francisco, which monitors and provides legal assistance for cases about the Internet and constitutional rights, has said, "State appeals courts have been developing case law in this area for more than a decade."

Greene said the decisions for cases such as these "require judges considering such requests to balance the needs of the person suing against the First Amendment rights of the poster."

Greene referred to a case in October 2012, when the owners of philly.com, the Philadelphia Inquirer, and the Philadelphia Daily News were required to disclose the name of an anonymous poster online. John J. Dougherty, head of Local 98 of the International Brotherhood of Electrical Workers, had sued the anonymous poster for defamation after being referred to as "the pedophile."

Dougherty subpoenaed philly.com's parent company, Philadelphia Media Network (PMN), to reveal the poster's name. According to court filings, on Feb. 26, 2014, the company was ordered to provide the reader's name and all of the comments that the individual wrote on the website from Aug. 10, 2012, through January 2014. PMN's attorney had said the company would not comply without a court order. PMN contacted the reader, who secured an attorney.

The attorney for the anonymous poster in court filings argued that the comments were protected by the First Amendment and were "not defamatory per se." The attorney for the union official said the defamation claim was "likely to succeed," but that they had no way of "communicating with [or] identifying the person being sued." As of late summer 2015, nothing had been publicly decided about the case.

Siegel, the lawyer specializing in freedom of speech issues, agrees that people who are offended should challenge those who post racist comments online. However, he does not think it can be considered a crime, even though some states do categorize racist speech as a hate crime.

"I think when we're talking about online comments, you could potentially try to make it a crime and unconstitutional," he said. "It's a high burden in the United States to win a defamation lawsuit. I'm a lawyer, and if someone said that I committed malpractice on a case and it wasn't true, and I was bringing in $300,000 a year, and then as a result of that it dropped to $50,000, I could quantify damage to my reputation. But very often, you can't do that."

An anonymous blogger from "Skanks in New York" posted photos of Armani model Liskula Cohen and said derogatory things, including labeling her as the "number one skank in the city." A judge ordered Google to release the blogger's information when Cohen was unable to sue the person without a name, according to the article "Skank Blog Case Puts a Small and Needed Check on Anonymity Online," in The Patriot-News in Harrisburg, Pennsylvania, on Aug. 30, 2009. After finding out that she knew Rosemary Port, the person who had said the nasty things about her, the model decided to drop a $3 million defamation lawsuit against the woman. Because she received so much negative attention in the press for her words, Port announced plans for her own defamation lawsuit against Google for $15 million, but there has been no new information about the case since 2009.

An article under the headline, "Judge: Reveal Who Posted Nasty Comment," Oct. 2, 2009, from the Chicago Daily Herald, detailed a case in which Lisa Stone, a Buffalo Grove Village trustee, objected to an online comment about her teenage son. The dailyherald.com and Comcast had to turn over the name of "Hipcheck16," the person who posted the offensive comment, to a judge. That case had not been tried. (There have been no updates to this case since 2009.)

Such cases should serve as warnings to readers that experts can trace what they write to their original Internet accounts, even if they use false names. However, it would require enormous time and labor for administrators of websites and blogs to identify the thousands of people who post racist comments online every day.

In one of the most prominent lawsuits about racist comments against African-Americans, black officers in Philadelphia filed a civil rights lawsuit against the city's police department, according to an article, "Philly Policemen Sue Department Over Racist Internet Postings," an Associated Press story posted on Grio.com on July 16, 2009. They had read racist comments on an Internet forum that they presumed to be written by white officers on duty and off duty.

The site, called "Domelights.com: the voice of the good guys," said the suit, included accusations that "black officers who get promoted must have cheated on their exams, included racial slurs and encouraged racial profiling." The suit alleged that the officers posted comments from department computers to the public Internet forum.

A white active-duty sergeant, who went by the anonymous screen name Sergeant "McQ" was alleged to be the founder and a moderator for Domelights.com, aka Domelight Enterprises, LLC. He was named as a defendant in the suit and accused of being a regular contributor who encouraged the negative behavior.

One comment among what was alleged to be hundreds of racist comments posted on Domelights.com said: "Kids, along with adults can't speak proper English or spell at a 3rd grade level, but they can sing among 'theyselves' the lyrics to a rap song."

Rochelle Bilal, president of the Guardian Civic League and then a 23-year veteran of the Philadelphia police force, at the time said: "Every time African-Americans do or say something in our city, we get this backlash of cops who think they're anonymous on this Web site — just racist, nasty, hurtful things about what we do."

The Guardian Civic League, other local chapters of the National Black Police Association and National Association for the Advancement of Colored People, and the National Association of Black Law Enforcement officers backed the officers who filed suit.

According to the complaint filed, existence of the website created a "racially harassing and hostile work environment" for the African-American officers, which is a violation of federal law. The suit alleged that white officers discussed the content of the website, made jokes, and said the word "domelights" in the presence of African-American officers, who knew it referred to the notoriously racist website.

Domelights.com was shut down one week after the lawsuit was made public with the message: "Until further notice, all Domelights.com services (i.e. forums, galleries, blogs) have been suspended. Thank you. McQ." According to the Philadelphia Inquirer, the accused sergeant, Fred McQuiggan, said that he "never encouraged racial comments, was not responsible for what registered users posted on the site, and never had been asked to remove posts or comments."

The case was settled in June 2011 with a requirement that officers be trained in antidiscrimination laws, review departmental policies on it, and take a one-on-one examination covering the law.

The case did not surprise Brooklyn Borough President Eric L. Adams, who cited another law-enforcement website for the same type of deleterious comments long before the domelights incident.

"We have police officers that have a site that's called NYPD rant, renamed 'Thee Rant,' and these sites have some of the most racist terminology, and at night they sit there and hide under the guise of the cybersecurity," said the former NYPD police captain and New York state senator. "That's the new Klan mask. The white hood of yesteryear is now the 'cyberhood' of today. They are able to put the hood over their heads, and that's the pattern of a racist. A racist wants to hide. The cyber universe is the best hood ever."

On "Thee Rant" (www.theerant.yuku.com), racist comments regularly appear, allegedly posted by NYPD officers hired to help people regardless of race. On the site, commenter "251430" on Sept. 7 (the site does not include the year) posted a rant titled: "The reason why shootings are up." The poster spoke about how difficult it was for an officer to make a "gun collar" or arrest a suspect for gun possession. The individual also brought up the Sean Bell case, saying that the department had no problem throwing its members under a bus, unless they were well-connected. The writer suggested that the Bell case was "over trying to get a gun."

Another posting on the same date made the discussion racial:

"Ok. Now that we've pussyfooted around the REAL reason and no one else wants to say it ... I WILL. Its because black people are violent, predatory, barbarians who are routinely given to homicidal behavior. At best they are loud, socially retarded and ill mannered. If my children never have to see one for the rest of their days, then moving from NYC will have been the greatest gift that I could ever give them.And I don't give a flying fvck who is offended by what I just said because I know in my heart it is true. They prove my point for me over and over and over again. In fact, they proved their social and moral inferiority 48 or so times this weekend. Keep on keepin it real playas!" – Posted by <u>WhiteDevil</u>-theerant.yuku.com

In today's bizarre cyberworld, it is probably much harder to believe "sticks and stones may break my bones but names will never hurt me," the adage of our youth, but the truth is that words have hurt us all for centuries. New York City Councilwoman Laurie Cumbo, founder and former executive director of the Museum of Contemporary African Diasporan Arts (MoCADA) in the Fort Greene section of Brooklyn, understands this all too well. On April 1, 2010, "The Local," a CUNY Graduate School of Journalism/New York Times blog, posted an article about "The Gentrification of Brooklyn: The Pink Elephant Speaks," an exhibition at the museum. The exhibition examined how urban planning, eminent domain, and real estate development were affecting Brooklyn communities, and how residents were responding to what is often a racially sensitive trend. Some comments to the blog complained about drug dealers.

"Maybe Ms Cumbo should take a short stroll down Hanson Pl, make a right on Fulton St. and after a couple of blocks take in the aesthetic appeal of dozens of young men actively engaged in the selling and buying of drugs. And realize that this scene is replicated ad infinitum. And realize that the pride she takes in her heritage is bespoiled by this scene and it's underlying violence." — Posted by Bangalore Borris, fort-green.thelocal.nytimes.com

Others complained about Cumbo's opinions.

"I have no problem with anything displayed or exhibited by Ms. Cumbo. However, she is somewhat disingenuous- her space is in a building bought and paid for with state funding, managed by a not for profit. The lack of debt allows her and other cultural institutions to occupy their spaces well below market value. To say that "not a single dime is going to a single black cultural center" [in Brooklyn] is, at best, ill-informed. She owes her livelihood to institutional support. While it is fair for her to criticize these institutions (even with hyperbole!) she should acknowledge her own contributors!" – Posted by IK in BK, fort-greene.thelocal.nytimes.com

She responded to this reader with a comment of her own, something she said helps the organization's goals of engaging with the community.

"Much of what I wanted to be accomplished in this exhibition was to bring about a mutual understanding for the need for change and growth in the community as well as a respect for what comprises the foundation of the community. I feel so challenged because I feel that those in positions of power to create change have not taken into consideration the importance of maintaining diversity. I went to the Brooklyn Flee at 1 Hanson Place on Saturday and I was amazed at how many of the vendors were white. Maybe about 90% probably more! The audience was about 95% white except for the security staff. I wondered as I walked through was this the new "ideal" look for Fort Greene. I wondered why would someone want such a monolithic feel to a shopping center when

New York City is known for its diversity? When people of power recognize that true diversity on an economic, racial, gender, age etc. is what makes a community dynamic then we will really live out the benefits of what this country should be based on. Until then, we will continue to implode." – Posted by Laurie Cumbo, fort-greene.thelocal.nytimes.com

Later, she told a CUNY Journalism School reporter, Inez Bebea, in a follow-up story, "I respond with my name, my title, my business, where you can find me. These people hide behind these nicknames and fake identities. It's almost like the KKK of the Internet. These people hide behind email nicknames, and they are able to go on and spit out this type of rhetoric without any information about their identity and who they are."

Cumbo, who was at the time running to represent Brooklyn City Council District 35, thinks comments on blogs are used mainly to gauge the "temperature" of a community by putting out inflammatory remarks and seeing what the response is.

"A lot of their remarks that you hear are so inflammatory that you wonder where are they really coming from," she told me. "And, do people like this really exist, that live on your block in your neighborhood and in your community? I think one thing that we're seeing is that with the creation of the Tea Party, that we're starting to see that these people … [have] been able to create and formulize a party. It's almost as if all of the anonymous *hate-sters* [her word] on the blogs have finally found some support and power and have discovered one another."

A party celebrating the release of Fox Searchlight's "Notorious" film biography of the late rapper Christopher Wallace, aka "The Notorious B.I.G.," in 2009 generated similar comments that indicate the haters have written African-Americans off as the most uncontrollable and wildest species of animal in humanity.

"Why are black people so violent? Why are they thinking of sex and crime all the time? They are raised to think such things are cool. Live by the sword die by the sword…if they would stop carrying weapons they wouldn't get killed so much. Want to prove how tough you are, try fighting with your fist like real men. And leave the punk weapons alone." – Posted by Zzsandman06, popeater.aol.com

When a 17-year-old Mississippi teenager died of an alleged self-inflicted fatal shooting at a traffic stop in February 2009 and his family wanted to know what happened to him, readers went off on a racist tangent:

"ALL YOU BLACKS THINK YOUR SO FU*KING TOUGH I BET I WOULD CALL YOU A N**GER TO YOUR FACE AND I BET I WOULD BEAT THE LIVING SH8T OUT OF YOU" – Posted by Kevin25872, fanhouse.aol.com

Brooklyn Borough President Adams, an advocate of cybersecurity, has hosted roundtable meetings with other politicians about the threats and solutions in both the public and private sector. He believes that the Internet presents the opportunity for airing a greater volume of hatred than was possible with other forms of communication.

"They are able to create not just a neighborhood stereotype where you have mid-western Klansmen isolated just to that geographical area of the globe, and they just had to find ways every once in a while to get a newspaper story out, now they can connect with folks with the same mind-set as them over the entire globe," he said. "They are able to shape opinions and negative stereotypes, and those stereotypes become the rule of the day. So we cannot be dismissive of what cyber hatred is."

Jerome Wright, citizen's editor of the Commercial Appeal, in his May 17, 2009, article, "Online Reader Feedback Helps Newspapers Build Relationship as Anonymity Lets Hotheads Pile Abuse," wrote that online comments that readers post on newspaper stories and opinion columns were just a part of "journalism in the 21st century."

"When online comments are abused, the result can be brutal," he wrote. As an example, he cited a story about a specific denomination, the Church of God in Christ (COGIC), that was moving its annual conference from Memphis to St. Louis. He said that readers wrote mean-spirited, racially tinged comments, which were removed from the site.

Said the Commercial Appeal's news editor, Gary Robinson, whom Wright had interviewed, "Unfortunately, a small segment of our readers chose to use the comments area of COGIC stories to vent their stereotypical and racist notions about that particular denomination. That's the negative aspect of posting readers' comments online, the aspect that raises the question of whether such comments truly represent divisions in the community and an authentic level of discourse."

Unfortunately, any community that attempted to have the types of "conversations" about race face-to-face that occur online today might immediately revisit the days of race riots. Writing online allows a cowardly racist to vent smugly, feel proud, and go on with his or her day after a gratifying experience.

Wright's story also included a quote by Carol Ann Riordan, vice president for programming and personnel at the American Press Institute in Reston, Virginia: "Allowing comments on stories enables people in the community to genuinely engage with their newspaper."

Riordan added that she was "amazed" at the mean and ignorant things people say. "That's why a newspaper's comments disclaimer is important."

That story suggests that Riordan assumed that newspapers could still distance themselves from the negativity by essentially saying, "We printed it, but we don't agree with them."

News sites that allow comments to articles generally have a disclaimer written into "Discussion Guidelines" or "Terms of Service" that says anyone contributing to a website, whether they are posting photographs, videos, articles, or comments, agrees not to submit inappropriate content. That includes among other points anything libelous or degrading to others on the basis of gender, race, class, ethnicity, national origin, religion, sexual orientation, disability, or other classification, etc.

In 2008, the Miami Herald site's language was a bit different, but meant the same thing. It said in part: "Although we do not have any obligation to monitor this board, we reserve the right at all times to check this board and to remove any information or materials that are unlawful. ...."

Although they might not realize it, a person who posts comments on any website is automatically agreeing to the policies of the paper, whether they check a box saying they have read any specific rules or not. Websites make it very clear that readers are responsible for their own content by saying, "You agree that you are fully responsible for your content," and "You understand and agree that we are not responsible for any user submitted content."

Somehow, both users and site moderators continue to ignore the part about degrading others, and many of those comments still appear online regularly.

Greg Moore, the editor of The Denver Post, in a 2014 interview for this book, said the paper began allowing limited access to commenting on their stories around 2003-2004. He said columnists and sports writers hate the commenting feature because people are so uncivil, nasty, and threatening.

"There's been a problem, of course," he said. "It's straight into racist, homophobic, xenophobic comments. And I just know what kind of stories are going to generate that kind of response — as black or Hispanic — and it's a terrible thing."

Moore, a former board member for the American Society of Newspapers Editors and for the Pulitzer Prizes, added, "And boy, do they get mad when you cut them off and when you tell them that they can't do that on our site."

Still, he thinks comments are important to have and are part of the paper's responsibility in helping to build a "sort of new town square."

"You want to write things that promote a discussion, and you also want to have a role in the community being a civil community, and it takes time," he said. "So I think it's important for us to do that and not shut off the spigot. I think moderating really helps."

"I think people actually go off more when they feel like they are being ignored, when they are saying things in a way to be provocative," he continued. "Sometimes it's just a reflection of who they are, but I find that as soon as they find out someone in the room is an adult, somebody from the organization who's responding or what have you, things get more civil pretty quick."

By 2009, the outrage against racist Internet comments had already begun, putting enormous pressure on the organizations to moderate them more carefully.

"The Internet is a reflection of the culture, and the culture is in an agitated state, especially where politics and race are concerned," said Nichele Hoskins, a former copy editor at The Birmingham News in Alabama. "The election of a black president has brought that agitation to a high pitch."

While working for a well-known newspaper in Texas in 1994, Hoskins worked with a white editor who considered himself a political liberal and assumed a "people are people" stance when it came to race. Back then, the newspaper was using public message boards that were powered by the Bulletin Board System.

"He often dismissed charges that the paper was racially insensitive or racist by saying that newspapers aren't smart enough to coordinate such a pogrom. When people on the editorial board pointed out the crap that came from those comment boards, he said that the boards were 'self-policing,'" she said. "He believed that the majority can maintain a civil discourse.

"I think that, to some degree this is true, except when some speech is deemed acceptable, or at least not offensive, to the majority," she said. "I think some very dangerous and offensive ideas are dismissed as just plain crazy talk, or as so outrageous that its offensiveness speaks for itself. But these comments never just wither and die. They feed off one another, as do the people who make them."

For most African-Americans, though, racist Internet comments are simply "business as usual." E. Ethelbert Miller, a literary activist, poet, and chair of the Institute for Policy Study in Washington, D.C., said the racist comments remind him of the 1986 film "Soul Man," in which the white protagonist darkens his skin to earn a scholarship designated for an African-American student. "The two white characters make racist jokes and comments, but keep saying 'no offense,'" he said. "But to me, it's what I see off-screen. Internet comments are a way to be racist in a very subtle way."

For that reason, he does not allow feedback on his eponymous blog, E. Ethelbert Miller. "I'm not part of the 'chatter.' No matter what you say, someone will disagree," Miller said. "Why open yourself up to that? It's not going to be anything insightful or give any information to grow. We should be using the Internet as a tool to build up the community. Instead, it's used to tear us down. It's a form of low-scale, Scud-missile terrorism."

Miller points out that some of the racism in comments may simply be the work of pranksters. "You could have a number of black people doing it to prank. It's like Internet vandalism to get it going, and you don't know who is black or white unless they say it. You have it coming from blacks as well as whites, particularly from blacks who don't 'see' racism. I call it chatter."

Miller suggests a simple reason why racist comments are thriving on news organizations' websites: "Newspapers are doing that because they're losing money, and are allowing comments like jock radio," he said. "People being outraged generates interest to the site."

When former governor David Paterson – New York's first African-American to hold the title, from 2008-2011 – complained that racist news media were thwarting his efforts for reelection, a NYDailynews.com reader wrote:

"C'mon people. Don't you know whenever a black person is not qualified to do his or her job, it's racism. Don't you know that when a black person is investigated for wrong-doing, it's racism. Don't you know that whenever a black person is arrested by a white cop, it's racism. Don't you know when a black person is de-nied a promotion, a job, benefits, or a hnadicap parking space, it's racism. Don't you know when a black kid gets suspended from school, it's racism. Just keep crying Wolf. Because nobody listens anymore. That's why this pathetic race has not advanced in 50 years; they're too busy blaming white people instead of helping themselves. Look in the mirror black folks; you're your own worst enemy." – Posted by smash44, NYDailynews.com

One reader commenting on the March 22, 2009, story about a paroled ex-con who killed three SWAT team officers in Oakland, California, suggested a way to stop black criminals with this:

"Here we go again, all black people need to be killed, forget about sending them to Africa. This is crazy, and we do hear about this everyday in Philly or whereever.White cops have to stop showing up first. Let some minorities get it once in awhile.This guy will probably get another slap on the wrist if he wasn't dead, at least there was some justice." – Posted by NJMike555, news.aol.com

Perhaps the most dangerous aspect of these types of comments is the mental and physical impact that it has on its victims. "They involve brainwashing and superiority," said Brenda Wade, a San Francisco-based clinical psychologist and co-author of the book "What Mama Couldn't Tell Us About Love," with Brenda Lane Richardson. "There is the myth of white privilege and the myth of black inferiority. It's very prevalent in cyberspace. The brain is a programmable tool. It loves patterns, and when you have that going on in a systematic way, it becomes a 'brain bundle.' There are 'brain bundles' with racism because of hearing it over and over again."

While it has been well documented that Web surfing can become an addiction like television and video games, reading and writing racist comments can also become compulsive behaviors and can be very traumatizing, Wade said.

"Racism is a serious health risk," she said. "Blacks are more likely to suffer both physically and mentally because of it. That's the impact because of elevated levels of epinephrine, which suppresses all the good hormones, because the body keeps saying 'run' or 'fight.' If you're white, you're reading and writing them. If you're black, it confirms for you that you live in a culture where you are not safe. It's very depressing. There's no way not to feel affected by it."

Janice Walters, an associate professor of psychology at Borough of Manhattan Community College, said a person who writes racist comments obviously feels anger and hate. They may also feel relieved or vindicated temporarily. Although she has never dealt with racial issues in her career and practice, she said that if she had to work with someone who was a known racist, she would try to help the person restructure his or her perceptions and thinking.

"I think I'd be helping them come to their own conclusions and make changes if they wanted to, because it wouldn't work otherwise," she said.

Keith Woods at NPR said: "White people or other ethnic groups who read these things about black people respond, I imagine, as they would in the larger society. Those with some multicultural experience or emotional intelligence will see bigotry for what it is. Others will find their ideas validated."

Whatever the subject, online readers tend to go off topic, and the more brutal the comments, the more their discussion-board peers seem to celebrate them. Often they get into verbal spats with black readers attempting to defend the race and defuse the repulsive language. These unfortunate protestors usually are drowned out by a cauldron of "rapid-fire" racial insults in a show of "one-upmanship."

In 2009, the Detroit City Council complained about racist alcohol billboards targeting African-Americans in their city. At the time, the ads had depicted a cartoon of the actor Billy Dee Williams holding a bottle of Colt 45 malt liquor with the tagline, "It works every time!"

Comments to "Detroit protests Colt 45, an equal opportunity high," an article published about the controversial advertising July 8, 2009, on walletpop.com demonstrated how verbal spats thrive online.

"Who else would drink that crap................." – Posted by Dave, walletpop.aol.com

"this is just getting ridiculous. Why do these people always bring racism into EVERYTHING?!!!!These are the people that are responsible for racism continuing to thrive. It's the people who claim that everything and everybody is racist that are allow racism to continue. If they would shut their ignorant mouths and just let it be, the problem itself would most like dissolve as well or at least settle down a bit. Stupid people. They really need to get lives. They claim that everybody and everything else is racist but the people who keep bringing racism up are one who are truly racist. Give it up you idiots" – Posted by james, walletpop.aol.com

"What next will come out of these black raceist mouths? Do they think big business is going to put a billboard of Afro Sheen or Jet Magizine in a predomintly white neighborhood? THEY need to quit being predjudice and come to reality that # 1 The reason most people in jail in big citys are black is because they are the Majority! You don't hear the people in Boise Iowa up in arms because the majority in their prisons are white. # 2 We owe them nothing. Our polititions in Wasahington appoligized for what some of our GREAT, GREAT, GREAT Grandfathers did. Get over it. They don't like the rebal flag and the whites don't like the black fist flagan so on . Why can't we work as a team to bring back the values and patriotism that has made our country the most relyed apon and stable country in the world. Tell Al Sharpton to shut up and help his people not to insite them." – Posted by Tom, walletpop.aol.com

It's hard to tell if this person who responded to "Tom" is black, but he really tells him off with:

"YOU'RE the one who should shut up... how can you blame "them" for speaking out? Who's going to do it for "them", are YOU? No matter what anyone else thinks re how necessary/unnecessary the outcry, people of African descent have no choice but to speak out for themselves. If, as you suggest, they "shut their black RACEIST (gotta love a self-hating hater's brain damaged approach to spelling) mouths", where the hell would THEY be today, you idiot? Nowhere. Same for the Jews; if they don't remind the world about the Holocaust and about the fact that it CAN happen again, and NOT just to themselves but to ANYONE, why... who's going to do it for them? YOU? Yeah. Right. Keep pushing your brilliance and showing how truly little you understand about the world. And learn, PLEASE, learn to spell. If you're a day above age three, you're one pitiful jackass." – Posted by George Ray Dorham, walletpop.aol.com

Someone else agrees with "James" by writing:

"James, I agree with you 100%. I've been saying the same thing since I grew a brain (and entered adulthood, where one can think for themselves and not just parrot what others say). It's the 'race-baiters' who propagate racism! Hear that? Again, let's repeat-- it's the 'race-baiters' who propagate racism! Next we must ask why they would do this? Because their livlihood depends on it! Most clear thinking Americans abandoned racism long ago. Race-baiters only serve to bring it back." – Posted by udavid1717, walletpop.aol.com

The takeaway is that black people should not complain about things that are offensive to them because racism is only in *our* minds and doesn't exist.

Perhaps the most disturbing aspect of online racist comments is how it affects our young people. According to a survey by MediaSmarts (Mediasmarts.ca), a nonprofit charitable organization focusing on digital and media literacy in Toronto, a majority of Canadian students think that racist and sexist comments are wrong, but think that they are just "jokes."

The national classroom-based study, "Young Canadians in a Wired World, Phase III: Encountering Racist and Sexist Content Online," published June 19, 2013, reported that out of more than 5,436 students throughout Canada, 78 percent of them in grades seven through 11 encountered racist and sexist content online. Although 78 percent of students told the organization that it was important to speak up because it was wrong, 69 percent said they thought people use racist and sexist language to pick on people.

According to the report, students have many reasons why they will not speak up: 57 percent said they don't say anything because they think the people writing it are just joking around, 52 percent agreed that people saying racist and sexist words don't mean to hurt anyone, while 44 percent of students don't speak up, they say, because friends that use the negative language with each other do not mean anything by it.

Fifty-two percent of students said, "People say racist and sexist things because they are insensitive, but not because they mean to hurt anyone."

These students aside, it's no surprise that complaints about racist and negative comments have increased over the years. Editors, publishers, and reporters at newspaper organizations seem to agree that the problems that racist comments are causing will not go away.

Days, the editor of the Philadelphia Daily News, said that racism against African-Americans is generational and something that we all grow up with. The fact that racist comments have become an extension of hatred that is delivered to the masses faster and to a larger audience is no surprise to him.

"But what gets on my nerves is that you don't want to think that it is really reflective of the average person," he said. "Are these people whom you work with? Are these people who manage you? Are these people whom you trust to manage other people? Are these the people who are making these comments? That's the part that's scary, but we don't know."

Jessie Daniels, in her book, "Cyber Racism: White Supremacy Online and the New Attack on Civil Rights," which Rowman and Littlefield published in October 2009, said: "The Internet provides no escape route from either race or racism. Instead, race and racism persist online in ways that are both new and unique to the Internet, alongside vestiges of centuries-old forms that reverberate both offline and on."

CHAPTER 2

Fear of a Black President: 2008 Campaign, Election, and 2012 Reelection Aftermath

"We are being blacked to death. Everywhere you turn the media is worshiping the half breed." – Posted by RebecRog3, news.aol.com, January 27, 2009

EVEN IN 21ST CENTURY AMERICA, the idea of then U.S. Democratic Sen. Barack Obama throwing his hat into the ring for the job of president was too much for some naysayers to bear. Anything and everything he did was subject to suspicion. His place of birth, his religion, his genealogy, etc., seemed to come under scrutiny because he is part Kenyan and a Hawaii native. Although most newspapers published positive and negative stories during various stages of his candidacy and presidency, it was clear that many readers could not stomach the thought of a black man occupying the White House.

Throughout the first campaign, a growing clique of "discussion board journalists" — as in readers hiding behind false screen names — unabashedly vented their thoughts about the candidate and about African-American people in general.

"My pastor told our congregation yesterday to Never vote for a Black man and I agree He will hurt this country" – Posted by Sjmc101, news.aol.com

Robert S. Anthony, the syndicated computer columnist and blogger, said, "The most venomous comments seem to come out when there is a newsworthy event like the O.J. Simpson, Rodney King verdicts, or the election of Barack Obama. On Election Day 2008, I remember seeing numerous online comments about how Obama 'will never be my president,' and there were plenty of hateful messages with the N-word and other expletives."

During the Obama campaign, then-U.S. Senate Majority Leader Harry Reid privately told Mark Halperin and John Heilemann, the authors of the 2010 book "Game Change," that as a black candidate, Obama would be successful because he was "light-skinned" "with no Negro dialect, unless he wanted to have one." (CNN politics/Mark Preston/Jan. 9, 2012)

The shock factor of hearing or reading such blatant racism about blacks has been eliminated, thanks in part to the Internet.

Sabiyha Prince, an American University anthropologist, said she frequently avoids reading racist comments from "cowardly," "hateful," or "ignorant" people. "It's disturbing to read, but it doesn't surprise me. It doesn't hurt me. It makes me mad. If you put it in the context of what we have been through in this country, it's just more of the same," she said. "While there is some historical continuity with these sorts of sentiments, there is something new about it to me. It is rooted in the resentment of Barack Obama and his presidency. It has tapped into old fears, some of which have been dormant. It's white insecurity that we are seeing.

"As an educator," she continued, "the thing I have a problem with, among everything else, is that it's so profoundly ill-informed and ignorant. It reflects narrow-minded thinking. It's not logical, and that's what racialized thinking does."

"RACISM? YOU'D BET! BLACKS HATE EVERYBODY !THE HALF ASS MUSLIM EMPTY SUIT IS GIVING US A BIG LESSON:NEVER VOTE FOR A RESENTED NEGRO WITH A DEEP INFERIORITY COMPLEX

!THIS PARASITE (NEVER HELD A PROFITABLE JOB) IS VOTING HIMSELF OUT WITH HIS ARROGANT STUPIDITY; EVEN IF ALL BLACKS AND LIBERAL MORONS BACK HIM UP, DON'T FORGET THE 50 MILLION WHO DIDN'T VOTE FOR HIM !" – Posted by Ardontarzana, news.aol.com

Mary C. Curtis, a Washington Post.com contributor and multimedia independent journalist, isn't sure whether these views should be stifled or freely aired for all to see.

"You go between saying, 'Should these comments be public? Is it doing harm? Or is it good for people to see these?'" she said. "After Obama was elected, people said it was going to be 'post-racial.' I don't know any black person who said that, because blacks were not naive enough to think that because this person was president that all of a sudden all the institutional, historical, societal, cultural racism, and also racially tinged attitudes, would disappear in the United States of America or in the world."

As a member of the Trotter Group of black columnists and a contributor to the popular column "She the People" for The Washington Post, Curtis says she does not get defensive about comments about her articles or respond to those who write them.

"It doesn't matter; you realize it's a certain mind-set that is disheartening," she said. "They make assumptions about you and your family and your upbringing, all kinds of things. It is almost like they are insulting everybody in your life. Being that I love my family and I lost my parents and had a great upbringing … it's almost as if even if you don't find it personally insulting, it just insults your family, your background, your ancestors, and black people in general."

In the days prior to Hillary Clinton's concession to Obama in the 2008 nomination race, the Rev. Al Sharpton publicly criticized Clinton for speaking about the assassination of Robert F. Kennedy. Any mention of assassination in the same sentence as the name of a black candidate for president makes those hoping to see the historic possibility brought to fruition uncomfortable, he argued. Because it was Sharpton who took Clinton to task, readers had a range of negative comments, and their fear of actually having a black president was beginning to show.

A NYDailynews.com article on May 25, 2008, "Rev. Al Sharpton urges Hillary Clinton: Watch What You Say," brought out the worst in readers who love to hate Sharpton and any other outspoken black leader, including Obama.

> "Is this what people want? Does anyone want this race-baiting **** and his homely racist mug in the white house? Here is Barack's mantra: My name is Barack Obama. Because I am part black you are not allowed to ask me any hard questions. If you do, I will whine and cry for I am weak. You are not allowed to question my wife's anti-Patriotic views even though she went to Ivy League schools on an affirmative action pass paid for by your tax dollars. You are not allowed to question that I sat in the equivalent of the black KKK church for 20 years and associated with every anti-white whacko such as Reverend Wright and Louis Farrakhan and Al Sharpton just to name a few. You will ignore it because it is okay to be a black racist and you should accept that but it is wrong or anyone else to question this. You are not allowed to turn your thermostat past 72 degrees, drive an SUV and you cannot eat more than someone from India because we need to care about the United Nations and what t (sic)" – Posted by Jason67, NYDailynews.com

When it came to deciding whether a white woman or black man was worthy of the coveted presidency, some readers automatically assumed it was unfair that Obama would garner the "black vote," which is odd since people who share their views also seem to love to point out that African-Americans make up only about 11 percent of the population.

One reader questioned how Obama could get ahead of Clinton in the polls since large majorities of blacks were incarcerated or barred from voting because they were convicted felons.

When Obama received the nomination, comments from many readers continued to be scathing. Other readers began to see opportunity in Obama's win, foreseeing the possibility of the complete elimination of "affirmative action" and the win to be used as the biggest example of the "lack of racism" on the part of Americans overall. Comments to the story "Voices of Color: Elation is Tinged with Incredulity," published by The Washington Post on June 5, 2008, clearly marked the racial divide.

"How can Americans of African descent be proud.....Obama was set up by Ted Kennedy.. AND now the DNC has rigged and thrown the candidacy to him!!!! We WILL NOT elect Obama the underachiever and underperformer. We WILL NOT ELECT Obama who subscribes to Afrocentric Liberation Marxist-based "theology" ....WE WILL NOT HAVE A BLACK AND A WHITE AMERICA!" – Posted by accountability_in_gov, WashingtonPost.com

Even the now-legendary "fist bump," which is considered to be a combination of a handshake and a "high five" greeting, between the Obamas as he declared victory in the battle for the presidential nomination on June 3, 2008, wasn't spared. This affectionate gesture (which may have its roots in sports or biker culture, actually) between a black married couple suggested that they could not be taken seriously, at least according to the New York Daily News headline "Barack and Michelle Obama's 'Fist bump of Hope' Shows Them Silly In Love" on June 6, 2008.

Some reader comments on the story conjured up stereotypical images of a black man:

"Has Black Osama announced what gang he is affiliated with yet? I'm thinking he has to be a Crypt. Does an Osama Obama presidency mean that Crypts along with Hugo Chavez, Mahmoud Ahmadinejad, Putin and Fidel Castro will be attending White House State dinners for special events on Freedom? Wow, the substitute teacher will be at the head of the biggest classroom in the world. Maybe Osama Obama can hire David Dinkins and Marion Barry as is advisors. "Don't diss your sis" Dave and "Crack is back" Marion can advise him on how to run his classroom. O' Canada......................." – Posted by uberchristian, NYDailynews.com

(Note: The reader might have meant "Crips," the name of a well-known gang.)

Four months shy of the election, The New Yorker published a so-called satirical cartoon as its cover of the Obamas as "fist-bumping terrorists." The drawing depicted future first lady Michelle Obama's supposed "revolutionist" tendencies, while solidifying the "angry black woman" stereotypical tag that had been attached to her early in her husband's campaign. In either case, many observers assume she and other black women are irate if they are not smiling or laughing. President Obama was portrayed as a Muslim terrorist.

While any political candidate is fair game for satire or humor, the Obama campaign condemned the cartoon as "tasteless and offensive."

In the New York Daily News' article about the episode, "New Yorker mag's 'satire' cover draws Team Obama's ire" on July 13, 2008, New Yorker editor David Remnick said in part: "Our cover ... combines a number of fantastical images about the Obamas and shows them for the obvious distortions they are. The burning flag, the nationalist-radical and Islamic outfits, the fist-bump, the portrait on the wall — all of them echo one attack or another. Satire is part of what we do, and it is meant to bring things out into the open, to hold up a mirror to the absurd. And that's the spirit of this cover."

One Daily News reader expressed his distaste for the president with this:

"Once a muslim, always a muslim. Obama is the sleeper cell we all were worried about. Everyone thought it was going to be a bunch of crazed muslims slaughtering innocent people. Instead, we get a muslim marxists running for president who a bunch of IQ challenged American people will vote for." – Posted by Cruzin, NYDailynews.com

When Chicago Tribune columnist Dawn Turner Trice wrote a commentary, "Obama must fight back but not with mud," on Sept. 21, 2008, it demonstrated that some readers thought that African-American journalists writing about black politicians couldn't possibly be objective. Readers were quick to correct her reporting with what they considered to be "wisdom."

"I do read your column occasionally and wonder each time what prompted the Tribune to give you such a prominent location in the paper. Is it your writing skills? In my estimation, you write approximately on a 6th grade level. Is it your wide selection of topics? You tend to promote racism as the cause of each and every issue in this country. Or is it becasue you are an african american? Yep. If we were truly a raceless society, your editors would not feel the need to promote this continued stereotyping. Your unrelenting support of Mr. Obama is very narrow minded and obviously race driven. Not sure how you face the world each day with this narrow view of life. You ask to get to the issues...yet you are stuck in the 60's wishing for your own piece of the pie. I on the other hand am simply a reader of the Tribune (for now) who tries to make fact based decisions rather than race based. Oh well." – Posted by Observer, ChicagoTribune.com

In the days leading up to the election, comments by the racist readers grew even more vicious, whether the stories were about affluent hip-hop artists ramping up pre-Election Day enthusiasm for Barack Obama or about predictions of the landslide victory he would eventually win. Most of the racist comments strayed from the topic of an article with lengthy explanations of why people should not vote for Obama.

"Hip-hop stars stump for Obama in South Florida," published Nov. 3, 2008, in the El Paso Times, dismissed those artists' directives for handling long lines at the polls with remarks that demeaned and stereotyped them.

"Are most hip-hop 'stars' convicted felons that aren't allowed to vote anyway?" – Posted by Ricardo, ElPasoTimes.com

Many voters in 2008 who arrived at the polls early found that they had to contend with broken machines and long lines that would at the very least delay their vote. An Associated Press story posted to AOL on Nov. 3, 2008, "Voters Across Nation Hit By Dirty Tricks," reported that the problems occurred in locations likely to have large numbers of black voters, and many readers vented their obvious fears about an Obama victory.

"There is too much RISK in having Obama as the leader of the FREE WORLD. He is out to make blacks above whites. He is out to side with the Muslims (blacks have a lot of Muslims in their midst) He will wreck America. Whoever takes the presidency from him in 2012 will have a difficult job bringing America back up to the Free Enterprise, Capitolistic sytem...we once knew an cherished.Obama is on is way to CHANGING America into a Socialst/ Marxist society." – Posted by BLevvintre, news.aol.com

With Obama's election, things turned uglier. Countless instances of Obama-bashing occurred during the first half of his presidency — everything from email photos of watermelons on the White House lawn and political cartoons depicting him as the gruesome "Joker" character from 2008's "Batman: The Dark Knight" film to the advertisement of so-called gag products such as Obama toilet paper.

These slights continue, but his campaign, election, and reelection helped to shine a light on other politicians' personal racism. They could now speak it publicly, so long as it was couched in terms of dissatisfaction with his actions or policies, not just his being in office. Later, they could claim that whatever they said was not meant to be offensive.

Richard Cebull, a U.S. district judge for the District of Montana from 2001 to 2013, forwarded a racist email that compared blacks to dogs and implied that the president's white mother had sex with animals. He later publicly apologized, claiming that he sent the email because he was "anti-Obama," rather than because he was racist.

Not surprisingly, the president's historic victory whipped up readers into a panicked and frenzied state, filling up discussion boards with hateful comments.

Days after Barack Obama's landslide of a win against John McCain, readers often used message boards and blogs to let out their frustrations over the election of a black president — regardless of his "triple threat" educational credentials, qualifications as an attorney, and political experience.

"i find it funny that ANYONE from a thug like state such as Ill. can chastise anyone else. This idiot elect was produced in that wonderful dump and everyone within its borders should just hang themselves." – Posted by tom9, NYDailynews.com

"Something was wrong with my TV yesterday as every channel kept playing the Planet of the Apes episode wherethe primates take over the White House. Very odd." – Posted by Phatbasdid, NYDailynews.com

One word that appeared often in reader comments after his win was "boy," which is considered just as offensive as the "N-word," "coon," "jungle bunny," or "porch monkey," among other racist words and phrases. Many remarks reflected a collective fear that a black president would see to it that black people got reparations for slavery.

"We just got a stupid BOY," – Posted by DonsANT25, news.aol.com

"Well, we're all screwed. There will be no oil for gas under Obama's new plan (which changes from day to day). Forget the elctric car, we won't be able to afford to electric to run it. Once he executes his plan to bankrupt the coal companies, we won't have any power for lights or heat. If you think that NO CHILD LEFT BEHIND is a joke, just wait Obama is going to hire a bunch of lazy black teachers to educate our kids. We know that they are lazy because we have de-segragation(sorry if I miss spelled it, I was shipped around town and educated by the black man). just wait until Obama implements his planned O.T.B. tax (other than black). It is a tax applied to all non-blacks for slave reparations and this time Congress will approve it. He will pick Supreme Court Judges who will say that it is prefectly legal. He will eliminate the constitutional rights of all OTB's because he and his church beleive that America deserves it. And we do. For to long have we cattered to the lazy black man" – Posted by NOS2001, news.aol.com

A new theme produced comments along the lines that President Obama would be exposed as a fraud like Jayson Blair, the infamous former New York Times metro reporter who had plagiarized a number of his stories.

Readers posting in the comment sections also found as many ways as possible to spell his first and last name incorrectly — anything from "Obuckwheat" and "Osama" to "Barracks" Obama.

In response to the article "Obama Shatters Barrier to Become First Black President," published in the Arizona Republic on Nov. 5, 2008, a reader named "Blogerrr" wrote: "Now that a supposedly black man is in office. Can we do away with all the racially insensitive programs like, Equal Opportunity and Affirmative Action? Someone help us -- Obama Osama actually believes all the hype about himself."

Comparisons of Obama to Peoples Temple cult leader Jim Jones, who led the 1978 Guyana mass suicide/massacre, helped other Internet trolls fuel the fires of hatred in ways white politicians would never be targeted.

"Remember, Jim Jones was able to get 900 people to follow him to Guyana and commit mass suicide. Why did they follow Jim Jones? Charisma? Message? Mental illness? Now ask yourself why all these people are literally falling over themselves to worship Obama, a man who has never shown anything but contempt for this country and the ideals it stands for. His background, if you would actually look into it, speaks volumes." – Posted by svierregger, WashingtonPost.com

Daniella Gibbs Léger's story on Essence.com, "Has Any Other President Been Shown Such Disrespect?" on June 19, 2012, made the case that throughout his first term, President Obama had to contend with heckling and verbal jabs that other presidents had never faced. I agreed with her because it seemed that his enemies were publicly saying, "Yes, you're president, but you're still black, we don't take you seriously, and we want the world to know it."

She cited the presidential press conference after Obama granted reprieve to undocumented young people who were threatened with deportation, at which Neil Munroe, a reporter for the Daily Caller, a conservative website, interjected questions before the floor was opened to queries. According to the Huffington Post, the president actually told Munroe: "Excuse me, sir. It's not time for questions, sir," Obama said. "Not while I'm speaking."

Gibbs Léger said that although the president handled the situation "like a pro and never lost his cool," she was disturbed by it, as other members of the press were. "Was I really watching the President get interrupted by a member of the press corps? Yes, yes I was. And for about 30 minutes, I forgot all about the substance of his remarks and the fact that the lives of so many young people would be changed for the better. Instead I was enraged by this lack of decorum and respect shown to Obama," she wrote.

In another example of stunning rudeness to the president, a congressman yelled, "You lie!" at him during a State of the Union speech, as if it were an outdoor venue. Gibbs Léger, a former special assistant to President

Obama and senior vice president for communications and strategy at the progressive think-tank Center for American Progress, took to Twitter to debate the trend of dissing the president.

She wrote: "So, I mentioned this on Twitter and I put it to you: Can someone point out a time in recent history when (1) a reporter interrupted a President during his speech — not during the back-and-forth of a press conference but during prepared remarks?; and (2) a member of Congress shouted out "You lie" or some other admonition to the President during the State of the Union address?"

Many of the racist detractors don't stop there. Some have even declared Obama to be the "anti-Christ."

"I really believe this Muslim moron clown is the Anti-Christ, as all of us will soon find out, and the prophecies will happen as foretold in the Holy Bible, as this man will deceive all of earth and lead us into Armageddon, and by 2012 it will happen, as all those Muslim/Arab countries that hate Israel will attack the holy land where it all will start, and it will all end where humanity began, in the Garden Of Eden in the country of Iraq. The rapture will happen in just a few years, and Christ will return to restore order on this planet, and then and only then wqill their be true peace on this earth. Barack Hussein Nobama Bin Laden is a dangerous man, but everybody is being fooled all over the world as you think he's some kind of saviour, but only Christ can save us. God help us all, total HELL ON EARTH the next 4 years, and there's nothing anyone can do about it, IT WILL HAPPEN!!" – Posted by LitlLucas, NYTimes.com

No other instance involving Obama was as outrageous as one that came in the aftermath of a story about a pet chimpanzee. The Feb. 17, 2009, New York Daily News story detailed a tragic account of a Connecticut woman's pet who was killed by police after the animal had mauled and critically injured its owner's friend.

The following day, the New York Post ran a political cartoon drawn by Sean Delonas, a senior staffer, on Page Six, that showed two police officers with an ape lying on the ground riddled with bullet holes. The cop with the gun in his hand said, "They'll have to find someone else to write the next stimulus bill," sparking outrage in the black community, as well as among people of other races who felt it was a racially motivated reference to President Obama.

Public backlash from the Post cartoon evolved into picketing outside the newspaper and threats of a boycott against the Rupert Murdoch-owned tabloid. Readers who posted comments supporting the Post feigned ignorance, claiming the cartoon was just an expression of opponents' aversion to the presidential stimulus bill aimed at bailing out banks and the auto industries that were drowning in the recession.

"Kudos to the New York Post! I am very concerned about the continued expectation of ethnicities that we curb our Freedom of Speech based on our 44th President's skin color not his race as he is the first to admit he is bi-racial. I'm tired of being labeled racist and blacklisted due to my beliefs that we, as a people, have constitutional freedoms. Poor taste is not covered in the constitution and yet the freedom to exercise poor taste is covered. So, New York Post I support your constitutional rights and long live our freedom to exercise poor taste!" – Posted by writerforhire, NYDailynews.com

On the day that the cartoon ran, the Rev. Al Sharpton told the Huffington Post, "The cartoon in today's New York Post is troubling at best given the historic racist attacks of African-Americans as being synonymous with monkeys. One has to question whether the cartoonist is making a less than casual reference to this when in the cartoon they have police saying after shooting a chimpanzee that 'Now they will have to find someone else to write the stimulus bill.'"

Col Allan, editor-in-chief of the New York Post, defended the cartoon and took the opportunity to take a dig at Sharpton, saying: "The cartoon is a clear parody of a current news event, to wit the shooting of a violent chimpanzee in Connecticut. It broadly mocks Washington's efforts to revive the economy. Again, Al Sharpton reveals himself as nothing more than a publicity opportunist."

On Feb. 20, 2009, the Post published one seemingly reluctant apology, later backed up by a more sincere version. Still, many readers debated the "double standard" because no one protested when George W. Bush was portrayed as a monkey by cartoonists many times after his election in 2001, and they suggested that blacks needed to stop making everything so racial.

"Where were all the outraged people when numerous newspapers, & websites posted pictures of GWB & a chimpanzee & said he resembled one???? Oh wait, GWB is white, oooops, silly me." – Posted by DILLIGAF, NYDailynews.com.

As Sharpton noted, it is ridiculous for anyone to think that any primate reference in connection with a black person is not offensive. After all the decades that have passed, how can one not know that fried chicken, watermelons, pigs' feet, witch doctors, blackface, malt liquor, chitterlings, chimpanzees, apes, and gorillas conjure up negative stereotypes about African-Americans, whether it is the written word, a photograph, a broadcast sound bite, or a cartoon?

"Yeah too bad Obama wasn't portrayed as the magic negro. The cartoon was depicting congress. But whoa, as soon as someone has the ***** to print a monkey, of course it means Obama. All the little liberals and blacks can't wait to identify themselves as monkeys so they can whine about racism. Don't come to my porch, you whining, crutch propped sad sacks," – Posted by gojiro, NYDailynews.com

Sharpton, students from Medgar Evers College in Brooklyn, the borough president, and black City Council members protested the cartoon by burning copies of it in a garbage can on the City University of New York campus. Many readers seemed to think that African-Americans tended to focus more on "perceived" racism, instead of fixing the many social ills that plague black communities. Brooklyn Borough President Adams did not agree.

"When you walk into my office, you see my poster campaign [geared toward young black men], 'We are better than this campaign': Raise your pants. Raise your image," he said. He's speaking about black men and the controversial sagging pants/baggy issue that has been a "fashion" style since the late 1980s, but has long been said to have evolved from the prison system's disallowing of belts to prisoners, which cause the pants to sag.

"Social ills are social ills, and I don't think one can be selective when correcting them," Adams said. "We can't replace one tyrannical or inappropriate behavior with another. So, I'm going to go after the chimp depicting Obama as a monkey being shot, and I'm going to go after the young man who's walking around showing his underwear. We need to be of a higher standard, and whatever it is, I'm going to attack it.

"When I come out and attack the New York Post's racist commentary, I'm at a level of comfort," Adams said. "I can also show the history that I also deal with, social ills inside my community — domestic abuse, child pedophilia, lack of quality education, lack of desire of employment, and I'm going to address all of those issues and I'm going to be consistent in how I address them."

The furor eventually died down, but the cartoon became one of many examples of so-called free speech slighting the president.On the same day the Post published the cartoon, the newly appointed African-American attorney general, Eric Holder, said that the United States "remains a nation of cowards" on issues involving race "despite advances that had been made." The story, "Holder: Nation of cowards on race," from Politico.com on Feb. 18, 2009, set off a maelstrom of reader comments, screaming for his immediate resignation and berating him for "biting the hand that fed him."

"Holder said that the country is now a "fundamentally different" place than it used to be, but that the nation "still had not come to grips with its racial past, nor has it been willing to contemplate, in a truly meaningful way, the diverse future it is fated to have" Maybe it is the black community that has not come to grips with the fact that they are expected to feed, cloth, house and take care of their own families. Slavery was abolished long before any blacks today were born. White man is not keeping you down. You get 12 years of free education, and in some communities, you get early child education. You have the same access to college funds the rest of us have. It is you that makes your choices, not me, not your neighbor. So stop using the white man as your excuse. We all have the same rights in this country." – Posted by TeamPolitico, NYDailynews.com

Seven months into his first term, President Obama found himself dealing directly with race after police arrested Harvard University professor Henry Louis Gates Jr. on July 16, 2009, in Cambridge, Massachusetts. The arresting officer was Sgt. James Crowley, a white police officer who was answering a call about a possible burglary. As it turned out, Gates and his driver were attempting to force open a jammed front door at the professor's own home.

After a verbal exchange, the officer arrested the professor on charges of disorderly conduct. Gates was held for four hours, and the charges were dropped a week later.

Asked about the incident at a press conference July 22, 2009, President Obama said in part that the officers acted "stupidly" in arresting Gates.

Some criticized Obama's statement and took it as the president calling the officer "stupid." Reacting to those criticisms, Obama said, "I have to say I am surprised by the controversy surrounding my statement, because I think it was a pretty straightforward commentary that you probably don't need to handcuff a guy, a middle-aged man who uses a cane, who's in his own home."

Crowley was quick to jump on those remarks. He told Boston radio station WBZ-AM: "I support the president of the United States 110 percent. I think he was way off-base wading into a local issue without knowing all the facts as he himself stated before he made that comment. I guess a friend of mine would support my position, too."

Obama visited the White House press briefing room unannounced on July 24 to say, "I think I unfortunately gave an impression that I was maligning the Cambridge Police Department or Sergeant Crowley specifically. … I continue to believe, based on what I have heard, that there was an overreaction in pulling Professor Gates out of his home to the station. I also continue to believe, based on what I heard, that Professor Gates probably overreacted as well."

The situation evolved into the infamous "Beer Summit" after the president invited both men to the White House to discuss the matter a few days later over beer in the Rose Garden.

Although the encounter ended amicably by all accounts, readers made their feelings known, in one instance rebutting "Anger Has Its Place," a July 31, 2009, column in The New York Times by Bob Herbert. Herbert took the stance that Gates was justified in his anger about a situation involving racial profiling. The columnist spoke of the need for black people to "roar out that anger at such treatment." He also said that the United States was not interested in "focusing a spotlight" on the injustices and "the urgent need to stop them."

"I'm not sure how much I believe all the complaints blacks make about profiling. A lot of it, including some of what's mentioned in this article, seems fairly subtle, and in any case the world is full of aggrieved ethnic groups whose members routinely exaggerate the offenses committed against them. Why should it be different here? But even if everything Mr. Herbert is saying is true, how important is it in the end? It seems to me that blacks have two huge problems that both vastly outweigh the profiling issue. One is the enormously high level of criminality in the black community, far higher than for whites. The other is their continued academic and economic underperformance. Both of these problems, in my opinion, are far more damaging to the black community than profiling, and it isn't clear to me that it is within the power of the white community to solve either. Could it be that Mr. Herbert is so focused on profiling because that at least is still easy to blame on whites?" – Posted by JohnB, Staten Island, NYTimes.com

Herbert ended on a somewhat controversial note: "Most whites do not want to hear about racial problems, and President Obama would rather walk through fire than spend his time dealing with them. We're never going to have a serious national conversation about race. So that leaves it up to ordinary black Americans to rant and rave, to demonstrate and to lobby, to march and confront, and to sue and generally do whatever is necessary to stop a continuing and deeply racist criminal justice outrage."

When Errol Louis wrote "President Obama, Henry Louis Gates Jr. and Sgt. James Crowley aimed to fix their mistakes," a column in the New York Daily News on July 31, 2014, about the notorious Beer Summit, he supported the meeting of all three men, whom he said had "been burned by one misunderstanding, determined not to compound the error with ill-chosen words."

One reader commented:

"Enough already. The fact is Gates is a black professor with a chip on his shoulder, Crowley was only doing his job, and Obama put his foot in his mouth and is showing his true colors, not to mention his inexperience. End of discussion, and this overblown issue." – Posted by The Wizard, NYDailynews.com

So much for the "teachable moment."

Long after the Gates incident, murmurings persisted among black leaders that the president was not doing as much as they had hoped for race relations.

In the NPR story "Black Leaders Ask: Where's Our President?" (March 12, 2010), Liz Halloran wrote that President Obama and prominent mayors and legislators across the country were part of a new wave of "post-black leaders" gaining prominence by the so-called trend of avoidance politics. She said both the president and Massachusetts Gov. Deval Patrick seemed to be moving away from the identity politics of their predecessors. Halloran added that "many" in the black community felt that the "historic" opportunity to improve race relations was "slipping away."

Members of the Congressional Black Caucus (CBC) reportedly were increasingly frustrated by what they saw as the president's "lack of focus on poverty and unemployment in the African-American community."

In September 2011, the president addressed those gripes at the annual CBC dinner, telling the attendees in part to, "Take off your bedroom slippers. Put on your marching shoes. Shake it off. Stop complainin', stop grumblin'. Stop cryin'. We are going to press on. We have work to do."

Both black and white readers wrote that African-Americans should be insulted and feel disrespected by what he said. Some said that he "dumbed down" his language when addressing black audiences and that he was an elitist. Others used the contents of his speech to "prove" to black voters that they had been duped into thinking that the president would be sympathetic to their issues.

"I found his speech to be utterly demeaning, out of touch and totally unsympathetic in a word clueless. Telling his own race that they should sit down and shut up when their unemployment level is twice the National average. Then he went bopping and jiving around the stage like a peacock. I don't which was worse, what he said or how these people are so race oriented that they actually applauded him This man hjas done ZERO for the blacks and they still support him. MLK said the Democrats would enslave the blacks and he was right." – Posted by DRGClarke, TheHuffingtonPost.com

Manning Marable, author of the Pulitzer-prize winning biography "Malcolm X: A Life of Reinvention," told Halloran at NPR, "It's not that America is suddenly post-racial. But there's just no such thing as a black president. Obama's base is multiracial and multi-class and a reflection of the reality of America."

Siegel, the legal expert on free speech, said: "I don't buy into post-racial since Obama. It's an interesting discussion as to whether President Obama has advanced [race] relations in America or at least, 'Did he advance it considering what we thought he would do, as opposed to what he has done?' And he hasn't done very much on the issue of race relations in my opinion. I think he shies away from it. ... In some ways, we're going backwards. America's still dealing with having an African-American male as a president."

As President Obama campaigned for a second term, many speculated that he might not win against the wealthy Republican candidate, Mitt Romney, because of widespread complaints that the president did not revive America's economy.

Seth Stephens-Davidowitz, at the time a Harvard doctoral candidate, presented research suggesting that racial prejudice may have had some influence on the 2012 election, both negatively and positively.

In a June 9, 2012, New York Times article "How Racist Are We? Ask Google," Stephens-Davidowitz discussed what he called "racially charged" Web searches and voting patterns of Americans who had gotten used to having a black president. Using Google Insights, a relatively new tool that allows researchers to quantify how often words are searched in various parts of the U.S., he ranked states and media markets in the U.S. "based on the proportion of Google searches that included the word "nigger(s)." He did not include searches for the word "nigga" because they applied mostly to rap lyrics.

"I used data from 2004 to 2007 because I wanted a measure not directly influenced by feelings toward Mr. Obama," Stephens-Davidowitz said. "From 2008 onward, 'Obama' is a prevalent term in racially charged searches.

"The state with the highest racially charged search rate in the country was West Virginia. Other areas with high percentages included western Pennsylvania, eastern Ohio, upstate New York, and southern Mississippi," he wrote.

Whether race cost or gained Obama votes in his reelection, the outcome spoke volumes.

In November 2013, Barack Obama was elected to a second term, which makes all of the negative comments from 2008 seem foolishly naïve.

Back then, online rantings about how the world was going to become "Armageddon-like," the president was the anti-Christ, and the U.S. would be so much worse under Obama's leadership all took a back seat at the polls. The consensus seemed to be that keeping a black man in office was somehow still better than having a new, wealthy, white Republican leading the country.

CHAPTER 3

Altercations With Police

"When is the black race as a whole going to start to take responsibility for their own actions ?? Their own problems and their own murder rate ?? Oh, I'm sorry, its our problem ?? Humanities problem ?? Damn, well you wanted your own Black collages, your own black Ms. America pagent, and even your own Black entertainment TV.. Explain to me again why I should give a sh*T why you (African Americans) "splinter the world" - for yourselfs, but expect us to help and give support and money to your issues... Sorry, you made them, you deal with them.." – Posted by JVSER, NYDailynews.com, Dec. 29, 2008

IT IS PROBABLY A GOOD thing that the Internet and the opportunity to comment on news reports were not so prevalent in the 1990s during some of the most racially charged events involving police officers. That includes the beating of Rodney King in Los Angeles in 1991 and the murder of the unarmed African immigrant Amadou Diallo in Harlem in 1999.

Sean Bell, the New York City bridegroom who was killed by police in front of a Queens strip club after his bachelor party on Nov. 25, 2006, with his wedding just hours away, became the biggest news story in the country. Police officers shot 50 times at the car carrying him and his companions, killing him and severely wounding two of his friends. Readers were able to conduct a verbal trial of their own completely online.

"F*ck sean bell and his hoodlum friends. Hopefully the rest of them die before they have a chance to procreate again. I say give the cops some medals." – Posted by Posted by johnie, NYDailynews.com

"I'll point some key facts. those cops were in the club for over 4 hours. Club policy is that purchase drinks regularly. So that means those cops in order to fit in, were drinking for several hours. Now when your at a club and you see several guys who you saw in the club approaching your car, the last thing you think is that they're cops. Also, cops are only to fire there gun three times and then evaluate the situation. This cop fired ten times the amount of shots." – Posted by speakthetruth, NYDailynews.com

"22heartfelt... the criminals that survived showed their true colors in court. don't rely on criminals to make this case... if anything, they hurt it." – Posted by truebomberfan, NYDailynews.com

"speakthetruth.. how do you know the clubs policies???" – Posted by truebomberfan, NYDailynews.com

"I would give odds on 2 of 3 convicted but I am sure nobody thinks all 3 will be acquitted or all 3 will not be convicted. Like the song goes "two out of three ain't bad" but I know that will not be good enough for Rev. Al. I can tell you for sure anything short of all 3 being convicted as charged will result in a protest but if all 3 are aquitted it will be called a riot for sure. I do not want a riot on my hands and would not want to be traveling alot around the city if one breaks out." – Posted by truebomberfan, NYDailynews.com

Not surprisingly, the officers who shot at Bell's group were acquitted, as were the ones in those other two historic instances of police brutality.

The Rev. Al Sharpton organized protests with Bell's fiancée, Nicole Paultre Bell, (who took his name after he died), and other black community leaders produced a nonviolent and peaceful protest. Yet readers who commented on the New York Daily News' articles published in May 2008 — "Day of Protest Over Bell Case May Mean Potential Nightmare for Commuters," "Quite the Civilized Protest Then," and "I'll Keep Protesting, Paultre Bell Promises" — poured salt in the wounds of the grief-stricken. Some gleefully expressed the hope that this incident would serve as a "lesson" to African-Americans.

> "Let's face it, these three were thugs. Their supporters are nothing but hood rat thugs with no jobs or responsibility. I can't wait to see how many of these protesters get arrested for outstanding warrents. The NYPD will have a golden opportunity to round up a bunch of thugs with outstanding warrants. Who else do you think will be there?" - Posted by NJDAD, NYDailynews.com

Another reader took a jab at the fiancée:

> "GOD FORBID she would get up and get a job to support her two little children. This is what you can do when you sit home waiting for a check and don't have to work for a living." – Posted by sean1030, NYDailynews.com

During the Bell trial, defense attorneys told reporters that the shooting was justified because Bell did not heed the officers' warning to stop his car, leading them to believe that he was trying to run them down. One irony in the case was that two of the officers involved were black, and so some people suggested that race was not a factor in the incident.

Months later, the Rev. Al Sharpton and other marchers were found guilty of "disorderly conduct" for the protests that he insisted were "peaceful." An Associated Press/AOL story, "Sharpton Guilty in Police Shooting Protest," reported on Oct. 8, 2008, that he was sentenced to "time served," but some readers posted negative comments about the community leader who now and forever will be a target for racists.

"Would someone please shoot this niggar (sic) in the head?" –
Posted by haywudublomee, news.aol.com

The dubious killing of another 17-year-old, Trayvon Martin, an unarmed
black youth, by Florida neighborhood watch captain George Zimmerman,
identified as a white Hispanic, on Feb. 26, 2012, provided an excuse for
readers to post hateful comments about black men.

Allison Samuels, a Newsweek/Daily Beast writer, wrote, "Where's
the Outrage Over the Killings of Trayvon Martin?," published March 19,
2012, on thedailybeast.com. Samuels (no relation to me) noted that celebrity activists such as George Clooney were protesting war crimes in
the Sudan and human rights atrocities, but that aside from the Rev. Al
Sharpton, few nonwhite celebrities were voicing concern over a killing
here in the United States. She was attacked by many readers.

"I have been following this story closely, and I've been very upset by it. I do not, therefore, feel the need to be scolded by Ms.
Samuels. Also, tragic as this event is, her comparison to the events
in Africa are--well, I wish I could say inappropriate, but ridiculous
is really the only word for it. I can't understand what she's bitching
about. She's mad because people are upset about children being
kidnapped, forced into slavery and murdered? Sorry, Allison, I'll
try to be more upset about what you say I should be upset about.
Screw those African kids. An American child has died!!! Whatever.
Oh, and Zimmerman looks more Hispanic than White to me. But
I guess in Allison's world only white men kill black men. I wish
I had nothing better to worry about than pretend race wars." –
Posted by PACman, thedailybeast.com

The author of the article probably never saw that. "I don't read the comments of people who write in. For me it's not very helpful," said Samuels.
"At first you might get some interesting critiques or things that should
have been said. Sometimes people might find a way to email me and what

they have to say is usually interesting and thoughtful and not really angry. ... My stories are based on my opinion. So if you disagree, you just have to disagree."

Samuels said the tennis diva Venus Williams once told her that she does not read comments that stories about her generated. That encouraged Samuels to come to the same conclusion. "I decided that I'm not going to read the comments," she said. "Unfortunately, on some level I'm probably missing something. I just don't have the skin for it."

It is probably just as well that she never sees comments like this:

"The author Samuels is another one of those shameless journalists that attempts to create controversy out of none to get suckers like you and me to click on the headline so the hit gets their site ad revenue. Looks like all that integrity they taught you in journalism school has been tossed by the wayside. The media is worse than lawyers these days." – Posted by CryConsCry, thedailybeast.com

Other journalists, including Commercial Appeal columnist Wendi Thomas, do not jump in to defend themselves when readers verbally attack them. "I have never responded," Thomas said. "I don't think there is any value to it. If I thought it would advance some higher purpose, yes. Otherwise, no. I thought I would keep the amount of negative energy to a minimum."

It is hard to discern whether black staffers at news organizations that publish what some consider offensive comments can remain objective in the face of blatant racism.

"I think there's precious little conversation about that in our business," Keith Woods said. "When I've had the conversations about these comments at Poynter, it's always been with journalists from a broad range of organizations, so I have no real experience in hearing from black people in any one organization. It's worthy of greater exploration."

Greg Moore, the Denver Post editor, thinks the dangers of racist comments aren't limited to just African-Americans. "I think it's dangerous for everybody," he said. "I think it's a reminder to us that there are people out there, whether they believe it or not, that think it's OK to be hurtful, and they use the N-word and things like that, or talk about someone's hair or whatever. They just do it to be mean."

Perhaps some of the people who write these racist remarks are desperate to "let it all out." It must be such a relief and elation for those who have been holding all of their racism inside of themselves all of their lives to be able to release in a way that does not come with public repercussions.

Moore puts it this way: "Because the forum itself feeds the devil in you just because of the very nature of it, you can be a person you are not normally. You can say things that you would not otherwise say. You can have a visceral reaction as many of us do to things. But they never give word to it. And they are able to do that online."

But Moore is clear on the fact that the words and language being used by commenters online about African-Americans do in fact elicit an emotional reaction from some people reading them.

"It's hurtful to see Magic Johnson being called the N-word in commenting on the Donald Sterling story," he said.

Sterling was banned for life from the NBA and forced to sell the Los Angeles Clippers team after racist comments he made to his biracial mistress about African-American men were recorded and made public.

"It's hurtful to see someone call the president of the United States a baboon or whatever," Moore said. "So that's hurtful to my daughters, it's hurtful to me and other people. But more broadly, that coarseness is damaging to the society in general. It just really is. I just don't think that mainstream news organizations' websites should be a vehicle for that. If they want to go on the KKK website and do that, then that's OK, but not for the Denver Post, The New York Times or The Washington Post or The Wall Street Journal."

For African-Americans with criminal backgrounds, reader comments never talk about how "intelligent" and "smart" black people are, even if they have college degrees. But when the criminal is white, the conversation takes on a much different tone.

After 24-year-old James Egan Holmes, a white man, killed 12 people and wounded 50 more during a midnight screening of "The Dark Knight Rises" in an Aurora, Colorado, movie theater on July 20, 2012, stories about him provided many painstaking details. The reports cast the young man as an academically gifted overachiever who had been under psychiatric care. White society seemed confused by his shocking act, as if higher education impedes criminality. Some readers seemed to have a difficult time comprehending how the suspect's seemingly superior intellect allowed him to become a mass murderer. Had he been black, many readers probably would have blamed his entire race for the crime.

> "He was a graduate degree neuroscience guy. He probably wanted to test the theory of the chemical interactions in the brain while committing murder. Remember. Everything these days is chemical according to science. There a chemical answer to everything and this shooter was an EXPERT GRADUATE DEGREE HOLDING human being on chemicals in the brain. He probably was using the theater a lab experiment. I know that's harsh to say? But it's a very plausible theory. When you're THAT SMART? Notice a pattern lately on these mass shootings coming from VERY VERY smart people? Outside that schizophrenic who shot the senator chick in AS, he too had a degree. I think we need a study on why very smart people are suddenly going crazy." – Posted by Michael Miller, via Facebook, USAToday.com

The movie theater shooting once again demonstrated the need for stricter gun-control laws. In the same summer of 2012, a flood of shootings in New York City's Harlem, Brooklyn, and Bronx neighborhoods in which children were among the victims caused black leaders to rally once again against violence and guns. When a New York Times story, "Living With Gunfire in the Background," on July 28, 2012, detailed the violence through the voices of those living in tough neighborhoods, some readers blamed the community.

"The root of the problem in the neighborhood that is the subject of this article is the continued problems of single-parent households in low-income and poorly-educated communities in America. This problem was aptly reported by the late Senator Daniel Moynihan, in "the Moynihan Report" written in 1962. We can write all the blogs, pass all the gun control laws and have U.S. Presidents like Obama for the next 1,000 years, but his is a problem, as described in this article will still exists, until most of the men who have children, in low-income and poorly educated communities, assume their true roles as father" – Posted by Claude600, NYTimes.com

Moynihan actually wrote that report in 1965.

When whites misbehave, no one blames the entire white race for their actions. Police officers used tear gas and riot gear at the Oct. 19, 2014, "Pumpkin Festival" in Keene, New Hampshire, an annual event attended by mostly white college students. Some of them got drunk, vandalized cars, and set fires, drawing comparisons to the Ferguson, Missouri, riots. The article "Why Pumpkin Fest riots are not like Ferguson," published Oct. 21, 2014, on CNN.com, discussed the "racist double standard" in media coverage and law enforcement response to the event. Donna Murch, an associate professor of history at Rutgers University in New Jersey whose research focuses on civil rights, social movements, and policing, told CNN in part that: "Based on what we know about Keene, the mostly white riots appear to have stemmed from alcohol-fueled parties. Ferguson is an ongoing, organized movement prompted by the shooting death of an unarmed black teen."

One Internet meme that spread throughout Twitter after the Pumpkin Fest was from "Bougie Black Girl" called "How the Media Works." It illustrated the thought processes behind how society views negative behavior by African-Americans and whites. She wrote: "White=Clashes, Blacks=Riots, Whites=Revelers, Blacks=Rioters, Whites=College kids, Blacks=Thugs."

Victoria W. Wolcott, author of "Race, Riots, and Roller Coasters: The Struggle Over Segregated Recreation in America" (PennPress, November 2014), was also interviewed for the online CNN story. "White behavior gets normalized," she said. "In the African-American community, the long-term complaint is that the behavior of a small number of people stigmatizes the entire race or community. But you don't hear that same racialized language about small groups of white people who behave badly. They do not stigmatize the community in the same way." Wolcott, who is white, is a history professor at the State University of New York at Buffalo.

In a decision released on Nov. 25, 2014, a grand jury found "no probable cause" to indict Darren Wilson, the white Ferguson officer who killed Brown.

Each year, the NYPD releases crime statistics based on race. The Daily News asked for statistics after civil rights groups claimed that 90 percent of the people shot at by cops in 2007 were black or Hispanic. According to the article "Blacks, Latinos lead crime stats-NYPD" on Sept. 18, 2008, the NYPD said that black New Yorkers were 13 times more likely to be murdered or arrested for murder than whites were. According to the analysis, blacks and Hispanics were the dominant suspects and victims of crimes. The report also said that it was because minorities accounted for the majority of crime suspects and victims.

From Jan. 1 to June 30, 2008, 244 murders were reported. Blacks accounted for 64.8 percent of the victims, Hispanics accounted for 23.4 percent of the victims, whites 7.4 percent, and Asians 4.5 percent. Of murder arrests, blacks were said to account for 64.9 percent, Hispanics 27.2 percent, whites 7.3 percent and Asians less than 1 percent.

In comments to the article, many readers expressed their distrust of the NYPD's findings and their views on racial profiling against minorities. Others used the thread to shore up the stats against the "doomed" minorities and to imply that if Senator Obama won the election, society could expect more of the same.

"It is unbelievable that after 40 years plus of all sorts of advantage GIVEN to these two groups, the animalistic and predatory behavior still lives within them. THEN the enablers and hurt feelings emerge. What are…the enablers and the offended defending? The government tries to help out, the thugs and low life's become dependent. Help to buy a home, they destroy the property and let it go into foreclosure. If they are engaging in criminal activities, the law can not approach them because then it is considered PROFILING!? Reading on a daily basis the stories of who is committing the crimes and WHERE should be to most rational and thinking people an embarrassment. Yet all the enablers and whiners do is BLAME SOMETHING OR SOMEONE ELSE! Expect more IF Robin Da' Hood [Obama reference] wins the election. People open your eyes and make the better selection, NOT that we have much to work with here that may have a chance to win. Things must change and this disease needs to be cut away and out" – Posted by AJM33771, NYDailynews.com

The "enablers" that the commenter is referring to are the government and programs that help disadvantaged African-Americans.

In 2009, four people were stabbed, one critically, at a Brooklyn club celebrating the screening of the film "Notorious," written by author and television producer Cheo Hodari Coker. The film was the long-awaited biopic of the rapper Christopher Wallace, aka "The Notorious B.I.G." and "Biggie Smalls," who was killed in a drive-by shooting in Los Angeles in March 1997. The stabbing after the screening in Brooklyn didn't make national headlines, but the comments about it were a lot harsher than the ones about the Colorado shooter. Readers attacked Wallace, the rap genre, and of course, urban blacks.

"biggie got what he deserved so did the people who got stabbed the worlds better off with all of them dead how do you make a thugh? Take one ape, give him a gun" – Posted by Nightowl1480, popeater.aol.com

Rap music with its violent rhetoric is often blamed for criminal behavior, as rock and grunge music have been cited as reasons for increases in white drug abuse and criminality.

"Hip Hop is a cultural bill of goods sold to America by its white owners of record co'sThere is no melody or harmony, just rhythm, so its appeals only to the primate urges, causing a violent response upon prolonged exposure.and mayhem." – Posted by Zzsandman06, popeater.aol.com

The New York Police Department was so concerned about rap's connection to crime that it set up an intelligence operation to monitor the industry. In 2004, Dasun Allah of the Village Voice chronicled the implementation of a special unit within the NYPD that focused on the rap music industry. His article, "NYPD Admits to Rap Intelligence Unit: A Look Inside the NYPD's Secret Hip Hop Task Force" (March 16, 2004), said the police force had a secret force or "hip-hop intelligence unit" to "gather intelligence" about the industry, drug traffic, gang activity, and incidents like the murders of Wallace and Tupac Shakur.

Publicly, the NYPD vigorously denied it, but a former narcotics detective, Derrick "Hip-hop Cop" Parker, told Allah, a former editor for the hip-hop magazine The Source, about the undercover operation, of which Parker was a key organizer.

"The pattern was that the rap music industry was becoming more like organized crime," Parker said. "It was running side by side with the traditional steps of organized crime. ... What interested me was I saw a lot of these guys that were really bad dudes in Brooklyn starting to latch onto rappers and entertainers. So I used to monitor the incidents, department-wide, of anything that happened."

His files included dossiers, databases, and photographs. He also did surveillance at concerts and other rap-related events. "The police department wasn't really prepared for the rap music industry violence," he said. "They really weren't."

After the revelations about the police intelligence unit, the hip-hop mogul Russell Simons pointed out in Allah's article that police did not follow white rock stars. "The police should be following drug dealers, not wasting your police force energy on singers," he said.

Ben Chavis, the civil-rights leader and then head of the National Association for the Advancement of Colored People, was also head of the Hip-Hop Summit Action Network, a nonprofit, nonpartisan coalition of leaders in entertainment, politics, and civil rights who use hip-hop for social change. In the article, he said the surveillance was similar to that used against the Rev. Martin Luther King Jr. by the Federal Bureau of Investigation during the Civil Rights Movement in the 1950s and 1960s.

"A very dangerous precedent has been set," Chavis told Allah. "It needs to be exposed, and we're going to take legal action against these police departments for violating the constitutional rights of hip-hop artists."

When it comes to race, hip-hop activist Harry "Media Assassin" Allen thinks the notion that rap is responsible for everything that ails the black community is bogus. "Rap music has given black people a place to talk, to express, to create, to observe those processes and those results," he said. "It's particularly done it for black males, who are often very silent. The average black man outside of hip-hop is not going to hear his voice amplified. ... Hip-hop created a place for all of that to happen."

He does see a difference in the way different races are cast in the cyberworld of commentary that routinely denigrates African-Americans. "Commenters tend to castigate the entire humanity of black people," Allen said in an interview for this book in 2012. "It just seems strange in a way, that when you have a mainstream news article that reports some given fact and then when you go to the comments, it's almost as if you put it on a racism meter. You have the articles, and they're kind of, like, level, and then it [the online conversation] just spikes and goes off the scale. It just seems like it doesn't even matter how innocuous the subject matter is. The comments become more explosive."

Allen has a point. In response to the article about the "Notorious" unofficial "after party," one reader, someone who had a lot to say about blacks, went "off the meter" in a rant that mostly had nothing to do with the topic, bringing up many stereotypes about African-Americans and especially men.

> "I think all blak people need to grow up and get a job. or as the blacks call it a j.o.b. they say it like it was something to be ashamed of. They should be ashamed to living off the white mans taxes and charity. They will never be a majority, they will kill each other off before that happens. They are better suited for living in Africa in a jungle than in a society of rules and laws. They no longer have a reason the reject the laws of the u.s. they have a representative in the white how now time to get your act together and start doing right for a change. They are mostly a bunch of tough talking scared punk girls who need their weapons to back up the fake appearance of strength that they try to project. The aren't all that tough withouth their knives and guns.scared little girls who dreamed of being men...the gun wont make you a man. Just makes you a scared black person who cant back up what they say without a weapon." – Posted by ZZsandman, popeater.aol.com

Allen, a former consultant to the groundbreaking rap group Public Enemy, said that not only are racist comments dangerous to blacks, but are also a symptom of something larger.

"My position is that we live under conditions dominated by the system of race, also known as white supremacy," he said. "White supremacy is a powerful and robust system that is profoundly capable of resource development, energy transfer, energy development, and it has all kinds of subsystems that keep it present and powerful."

He must have had in mind comments like these:

"Pass out more knives to a larger population of blacks on Medicaid and Welfare, that is how we get out of this economic mess. Let them kill each other. It is that simple." – Posted by Mulva999, popeater.aol.com

This comment was in response to the "Notorious" film screening. It went far off topic and suggested that as long as blacks keep killing each other, the state would not have to spend as much money on programs to help them.

CHAPTER 4

Black Women: Bad Choices?

"Stop spreading your legs for every new stud and give yourself a chance to make it in this society ! Be responsible for your actions! Society is tired of footing the bill for your indiscretions!" – Posted by VERITAS, MiamiHerald.com, May 7, 2008

An Oct. 28, 2008, article, "Jennifer's Tragedy Hits us Where We Live, Too Many Moms Are Quick to Defend their Troubled Sons," by Chicago Sun-Times columnist Mary Mitchell, was one of many stories about the deaths of singer and actress Jennifer Hudson's mother, brother, and nephew. They were killed by Hudson's sister Julia's ex-husband, William Balfour, that Oct. 24.

As with many comment threads in response to situations involving a black man and woman, the dialogue almost always brands the latter as the stupidest human beings on the planet.

> "The problem in the Black Community is that unattractive Black women think that they must have a man, any man, to be fulfilled. So you have these huge, overweight, low self-esteem Black women hooking up with ex-convict scumbags, in which the scumbags don't care about these women—they only want to use these women to take financially care of them. These idiot Black women bring these scumbag men into their family settings, and these low-life's hate the women's families. I speak from personal experience, as

my sister was neither fat nor ugly, but was drop-dead gorgeous as a young woman. She hooked up with a military deserter who had did time in a military prison. My sister was stupid, and because this was toward the end of Viet Nam, and my sister was a lefty-peacenik, she felt sorry for this scumbag and he almost ruined my sister's life. My entire family hated the guy, and I was the eldest son in the household and wouldn't let the scumbag come by our home. This guy knew I would have "popped him" in a minute—and I only would have had to complete tons of paperwork after the deed was done.The guy died from a drug over-dose a few years later, a person that society would never miss. What these unat-tractive Black women must realize is that if a normal, law-abiding regular guy doesn't want to date you, why would an ex-con want you? Only to use you. These women must learn to respect and live with themselves, and if it means alone forever, so be it. Stop bring-ing these low-life, scumbag, convicts into your families' homes and lives." – Posted by JohnnyQ, SunTimes.com

In recent years, the "war on women" has become an often-used politi-cal catchphrase that commonly means the restriction of women's rights via funding and policies on reproductive rights, workplace discrimination, and violence. In online communities, a deliberate, targeted, and tactical "war" against African-American women has been gaining momentum. It infuses the media with old and new stereotypes. The conflict centers mainly on a single black woman's decision to have a child, her choice for a mate, and the number of children she has.

Black women's choices seem to be more heavily scrutinized than other women's are. Whether news stories are about a domestic situation be-tween black couples or teen parents, reader responses tend to be brutal, cruel, and racist. The discernment is that black women lack integrity and discipline, are incapable of caring for their own children, and prefer gov-ernment assistance to employment. The story below was a bit different, but earned the same type of response.

On Oct. 18, 2007, Natavia Lowery, who was 28, was arrested and charged with killing "celebrity" realtor Linda Stein, her employer, by bludgeoning her with a yoga stick. Lowery claimed that it was because Stein was abusive to her. What pushed her over the edge, she said, was that Stein kept blowing marijuana smoke in her face and making vague racial remarks.

Lowery originally confessed to the crime, but then said that her confession was coerced. At trial in 2010, it was alleged that Lowery had stolen money from Stein and had a history of financial misdeeds. The accused woman, who gave birth to a child during her trial, was found guilty and sentenced to 30 years to life.

Some of the people who commented to news articles about the case responded with some levels of sympathy, specifics on the case, and advice. Most of the negative comments, however, centered on Lowery's reproductive status:

> "This low-life savage needs to be sterilized, so that she can't contaminate the world with more murderers;oh ****, she already has. I guess in her warped little mind,she was just blowing off a little steam,trying to get rid of stress." – Posted by kerryman35, NYDailynews.com

And there you have it — the fear that any future child of Lowery's — will grow up and murder more white people.

Many comments that appear attached to articles in media offer specific "rules" for black women to follow, including choosing "regular" guys to date and learning to accept as their destiny that they will be alone for the rest of their lives.

Even black men use this as ammunition against black women. Many comments about black women's relationships with black men stir up a pot of bitterness, further amplifying the myth of historic divisiveness between black men and women. In the New York Daily News story about Hudson's tragedy, one man, presumably black, told black women off with this:

"I've got to chastise the ignorant women who love the hip hop ghetto lifestyle and perpetuate it by loving no good gangsters. There are many hard-working, albeit poor, black men who ask you out still you opt for the 'excitement' of getting with gansters. They are not better men than us 9 to 5 stiffs, nor are they more physically endowed yet you bring these losers into your life and among the family members who love you, thus stupidly putting their lives at risk. The worst thing is that Jennifer Hudson's alarmingly obese sister will go to her grave not having the tiniest idea of how she contributed to this and will never take responsibility to this great loss. Hate to admit it but today's 'modern' black women are dangerously dumb when it comes to men & their vision of the ideal mate. And they'd rather convince themselves that they know it all than to humble themselves & give up this urban romance novel fantasy of "thug love." In real life thug love leads to pain, suffering and death. Wake up, Black Woman." – Posted by Blacknproud, NYDailynews.com

Ingrid Sturgis, a former editor of Essence.com and AOL Black Voices.com and now a tenured professor of communications at Howard University who specializes in social media trends, has noticed this trend.

She said in an interview for this book: "Racist comments against black women are really a shame, because we really haven't gotten over a lot of issues from slavery. It seems we really haven't resolved any of those issues. Just when we think we have gotten over things, it pops up again."

These comments make it seem as though black women have a large, untapped pool of hardworking, "regular" black men from whom to choose. This rant was in response to the New York Daily News story "Queens woman, sons rescued after jilted boyfriend set her on fire," published Nov. 16, 2009, by a self-identified black man:

"This happens when black women continue to fall madly in love with career criminals. Most black men have been arrested in life but some decide that prison is not for them and learn their lesson. Alas the "sistas" spurn them as potential mates for the excitement of loving repeat offenders. Then they bring these punks around their kids to get at the biological dad. If the "sistas" took responsibility for their choices, they would not have the "bad man" to blame in the first place. Wake up" – Posted by Blacknproud, NYDailynews.com

This reader doesn't mention where he fits in the grand scheme of things, but he sounds as though he is speaking from personal experience. It's like he's saying a man who has some jail time but considers himself rehabilitated is better than another who keeps getting in trouble. It's hard to imagine that there is competition between those two categories. In either case, black women do not escape being targeted for any decisions they make.

Professor Sturgis admits that black people have a lot of issues.

"We're in a society that has created genocide against black men," Sturgis said. She is also the author of "The Nubian Wedding Book: Words and Rituals to Celebrate and Plan an African-American Wedding" (Crown, 1997), editor of "Aunties: Thirty-Five Writers Celebrate Their Other Mother" (Ballantine Books, 2004), and co-editor of "Social Media: Pedagogy and Practice" (University Press of America, 2013).

"Black women can't find black men," Sturgis added. "The black women are blaming black men for their lack of money and education. The black women and men are fighting, and the black race is vulnerable because the entire black family structure has broken down. Something integral has been done, and I don't know if anything can be done to resolve it."

As if we do not have enough going against us, the pontifications about the black women's "marriage crisis" have become lucrative fodder for talk shows on television and radio that use old statistics to ramp up fear and anxiety among black women. The clear-as-day message to the public is that black women are unwanted, unloved, undateable, and unmarriageable.

A reader responding to the New York Times article "Blacks Need to Reinvent Marriage," published Dec. 20, 2011, offered an insulting comparison with this comment:

"The reason there are no suitable black men for the black women to marry is anything new. The reason is that black men are never well raised, well enough to be marraigble. By "well raised" I mean, educated, relationship ready— men without severe personality disorders or narcissistic or sociopathic or criminal behaviors. Men have to be able to relationship ready and live in families and enjoy children and a good family life. But what's happening is that without mothers at home especially most male children develop serious learning or personality disorders— these issues that cannot be fixed at schools, in group setting. It's like a famer who never tilled or prepared the ground, planted seeds or nurtured plants and raised crops for a healthy and bountiful harvest— asking where my bounty of crops is. Most women in America black or white don't have children or put enough effort to raise them well. For that reason they will deprive the next generation of American women of good husbands. This situation has existed among blacks for a generation. Now it is happening with whites as well. It's becoming harder and harder for educated white woman to find a suitable partner, these days. Most have to marry below themselves just like most black women have done for generations. So that it appears black people have not become like white people after all in America, like our big liberal politicians fantasied, but the reverse is true, that white people are increasingly becoming like black." – Posted by jcfish, seattle, WA, NYTimes.com

According to Jenée Desmond-Harris of The Root, two academicians have dispelled some of the myths about black marriage using old Census records and the bureau's American Community Surveys.

Ivory A. Toldson, a Howard University professor and Congressional Black Caucus Foundation research analyst, and Bryant Marks, a psychology professor at Morehouse College and faculty associate at the University of Michigan's Institute for Social Research, did the independent analysis that clarifies the statistics.

Harris interviewed the two men for an Aug. 18, 2011, article, "Myth Busting the Black Marriage 'Crisis.'"

One statistic that is often cited is that more than 40 percent of black women are single and unlikely to find husbands. Using American Community Survey data from 2000-2009, they found that among black women 35 and older, the percentage that have never been married drops to 25 percent. A solid majority (75 percent) of black women get married before they turn 35.

"The often-cited figure of 42 percent of black women never marrying includes all black women 18 and older," Toldson told Harris. "Raising this age in an analysis eliminates age groups we don't really expect to be married and gives a more accurate estimate of true marriage rates."

The scholars also called into question the notion that successful black men are in short supply and unavailable to black women because the men prefer to marry outside of their race. Overall, Toldson and Marks give a solid message to the black community that essentially says to "scrutinize the agenda of the media" that revel in the grim statistics about black relationships and marriage.

While the pair admit that black women have received more degrees than black men since the 1960s, Toldson and Marks said more black men than black women earn more than $75,000 per year, and that black men are twice as likely to earn salaries above $250,000. "Success" among black men, they add, is something that should be examined more broadly. The fact is that education does not always determine income.

"Entrepreneurial elements of America have found a variety of creative ways to benefit financially from black females' anxieties at the expense of black male egos," Toldson said.

Those who post racist comments on news stories have exploited these issues to press their points of view. While it may be no one's business, many commenters seem to enjoy making crass jokes about whether the children of black women mentioned in articles have a father in their lives. If they do not — and even when the observer does not know if that is the case — readers are quick to offer their idea of solutions, which often include ways to stop black women from having children.

In Dallas, Texas, a black woman who had five children was accused of helping to cause the death of her 9-year-old diabetic daughter by not controlling her sugar intake. According to the article "Mother Charged in Diabetic Girl's Death," Feb. 4, 2009, on AOL/Associated Press, the child was said to have died lying "beside bags of candy and other sweets."

The woman's husband came to his wife's defense, saying that she was a good mother and a good woman. Although she was married and her husband lived in the same house, readers berated her with the type of dialogue normally seen in response to stories that identify single mothers:

"Wonder if she'll even care, except for the subtracted amount off her check every month. Better pop out a new one to get the total back up there." – Posted by Heatseaker22, news.aol.com

Complaints about this black woman's marital status should not have even been a part of the comment thread for this story, but many readers vented heir disbelief that the accused woman actually had a husband who was living in the home with his wife and children.

"The father? People like this don't know who or where the father is. She'll be having another kid in a few years again I'm sure. Mandatory sterilization is the only way to go in cases like this OR life without parole." – Posted by Bobpe11, news.aol.com

The underlying message is that it doesn't matter if black women follow the "rules," nothing she does is ever going to be good enough for society to view her favorably. If a black woman has children out of wedlock, she is considered to be stupid, promiscuous, and sex-crazed. If she gets into a relationship with an alcoholic or an abusive man, she's perceived as stupid and suffering from low self-esteem for not making a better choice. If a black woman is on welfare or getting any financial help from Social Services, she is said to be stupid, ignorant, and lazy. The list goes on and on. If she is involved with a man who is not working, but she is, then she is perceived to be "desperate."

The focus never seems to be about why men of all races run away from fatherhood. The discussion also seems limited to the mere presence of the father in the physical sense and his ability to provide material things, not about whether he plays a role in the child's development emotionally and intellectually.

Responding to an article that put a positive spin to an age-old issue, readers lambasted young grandmothers in the New York Daily News article "Thirtysomething Grandmas Have High Hopes for Daughters' Futures," published May 8, 2008. Most readers who commented generalized that the grandchildren were all born through Medicaid and that the grandmothers were getting welfare benefits to pay for them.

> "Young girls getting pregnant on my dime! I don't care how fashion conscious they are, these ****** should be ashamed of their lives! They had sex and resulted in a ******* being born and guess what? We pay for these babies! You would think that they would teach their children not to make the same mistake but they do the same thing! Where are the sperm donors? Why do we always have to pick up the care of these stupid girls? These girls are never married to these guys and its no wonder when they have multiple babies with these whores! There is no consequence to humping them!" – Posted by mbdono, NYDailynews.com

Ironically, when it was learned that then-Republican vice presidential nominee Sarah Palin's 17-year-old daughter, Bristol, had become pregnant and was unmarried, Palin supporters let her have a pass because the father was planning to be a responsible parent. Once out of the spotlight, Bristol and her former fiancé ended their relationship, not unlike scores of teen and adult couples of any race.

Readers prefer to act as judge and jury, however, when it comes to black teen girls who become pregnant. Brenda Wade, the San Francisco psychologist and author, said that some of the negative perceptions of young black women come from images reflected in hip-hop lyrics and music videos. Although not a new theory, the effects of a genre of music and culture that began in the early 1980s prove that its damage to black communities is unending, as seen through Internet comments some 20 or so years later.

"The brain is not complete until 24 years of age," Wade said. "Rappers came into the industry with incomplete brains, and they have become un-witting tools. Hip-hop lyrics are repetitive with a lot of emotional inten-sity, which the brain loves. All they have to do is call women bitches and hoes, and they can get paid for it."

The hypocrisy is that at the same time, the very same women being called derogatory names are the "baby mamas" that are being assaulted by society's contradictions when the men, whose images reflect rappers, do not live up to their end of the bargain in relationships and parenting.

Comments to the April 17, 2008, article "Stunned Mom Gets Tot Back" included a frenzy of responses about a woman whose child's father took their baby at gunpoint. Although she had an order of protection against him, readers dominated the threads with cynical and mean opin-ions. Some of them, like the one below, cast the mother as the root cause of her own problems:

"This hallowed young angel of a mom chose to sleep with a dead-beat criminal type whom she knew had no money. She could then hang around exciting 'bad boys' who distracted her from her own dead-end life. A man can never choose parenthood as an option, but it is always available to a female. This enabled her to start her career as a welfare mother, and as a career Victim. Instead of finishing high school, refraining from getting pregnant, and making something out of herself (which requires a lot of work!), she Chose the easy way out: getting k n o c k e d up. I only feel sorry for the baby." – Posted by footstool, NYDailynews.com

The rants never take account of conditions and disparities that are beyond the control of the young women or the young men. For Councilwoman Laurie Cumbo, founder of the Museum of Contemporary African Diasporan Arts (MoCADA) in Brooklyn's Fort Greene section, working at a nonprofit affords her the opportunity to have a behind-the-scenes view of the disparities in funding for specific communities. "The inequities in the ways our communities are funded have such a gross impact on our educational system. It has a gross impact on our relationships, on our ability to find jobs, on our ability to raise our families. All of these things are directly related," she said.

Since community centers and educational programs to keep black children engaged are often scarce, they end up bored and prone to search for comfort and or excitement. Today, video games and the Internet serve as babysitters, and parents are overwhelmed and exhausted.

"All these things are cycles. People start getting to the standpoint where they're saying black women are having too many children, and they'll marry anybody, a bum, a homeless person," said Cumbo, who resigned from her museum post to run for a seat on the New York City Council. "But when you're on that level making those types of statements, you're still at the bottom of the totem pole of intellectual thought because when you're here thinking about that kind of thing, you are so unaware of all levels of power in the chain of command that are so far ahead of you."

When then-presidential candidate Barack Obama gave a frank discussion on fatherhood directed at the black community, readers still were not satisfied. The New York Times' "Obama Calls for More Responsibility from Black Fathers," June 16, 2008, raised issues of class, gender, and interracial coupling:

"It was Obama's 'Sister Souljeh' moment, carefully crafted for the wider audience. It would have done more good had he seen to it that this sermon was preached sometime in the 20 years he sat in the pew and listened to Jeremiah Wright spew his hate filled messages." – Posted by Wendy, Vienna, VA, NYTimes.com

"Males, black or white, are afforded equal opportunity to out earn women. I am tired of hearing how oppressed African-Americans, who have never seen Africa, have it in this country. Anyone running for the White House better call themselves American and leave Africa to the Africans." – Posted by Teri Towse, Alton Ill, NYTimes.com

The discussion should be about how children are the future of our society and what we must do to help them have happy childhoods and ascend into fruitful adulthood. If one were to take to heart what readers think about black children, it would be that they are failures before their parents' sperm and ova join. Readers of the June 11, 2008, article, "Kyle Smith Was Happy in New Home — ACS" in the New York Daily News detailed the events that led to a child being beaten to death while in the custody of a female guardian and her boyfriend. The child's mother, who was said to be a drug addict, left him with the guardian, who had initially received satisfactory reports from the Administration of Children's Services. Some readers responding appeared to blame the woman more for her choice of a mate than for the horrendous act itself.

"MOST black kids are NEVER going to have two parents because a lot of black women don't think or care about who they make their 'baby daddy'. They will take pimps, drug addicts, prostitutes, the unemployed, the crippled, and the homeless. They don't care. All they want to be able to say is that they 'got a man'. As a black male whose mother is a high school principal, and whose father is a drug addict, I can tell you, a large percentage of black women fail to realize that their responsibility to their child begins BEFORE conception, with picking an appropriate father." – Posted by sean1030, NYDailynews.com

Tragedy, despite affluence or notoriety, can hit home. The Oscar-winning singer-actress Hudson lost three generations of her family — her mother, brother, and nephew, allegedly at the hands of her sister's ex-husband. Nephew Julian King, who was just 7 years old, had been kidnapped and was found dead in a parked SUV days after his grandmother and uncle were shot to death in their home. Readers responding to the story "Jennifer's Tragedy Hits Us Where We Live, Too Many Moms Are Quick to Defend Their Troubled Sons," by Chicago Sun-Times columnist Mary Mitchell, criticized Julia Hudson's choice for a mate and her decision to raise her family in Chicago.

The award-winning journalist, who is also an advocate for women, wrote about how mothers of criminals often try to shield them, regardless of tangible proof of wrongdoing. Mitchell detailed killer Balfour's record, which included parole violation, attempted murder, vehicular hijacking, and possession of a stolen car.

"It goes without saying that he's innocent until proven guilty," Mitchell wrote. "But any reasonable person would understand why police went looking for him. Wake up, mothers."

What also sparked a nerve with readers was how Julia Hudson's mother-in-law publicly defended her son.

Michele Davis Balfour, the mother of Julia's ex-husband William Balfour, said, "My son had nothing to do with this," and "I'm very upset with police because they are refusing to let me see my son."

Mitchell pointed out that despite Balfour's criminal history; his mother seemed to be upset only that her son was being unfairly profiled.

"No one wants to say it but this is Julia's fault! You don't bring men like this around your family and child! This looks like an execution so I don't believe that William did this but I do believe that he owed someone some money, which is why20he sold the car, and they came back to where he was staying, at the mother's house, and blasted everyone in the house. Julia knew he was a criminal but because of her weakness for good d!ck (her words, not mine), she put her baby in this situation. Julia knew her man owed these people. Just wait for it all to come out. I do agree that mothers need to stop coddling their sons but in this case, that woman is right. He didn't do this. The people he owed did this and that's why he's in PROTECTIVE custody. Why else wouldn't they release where he is? Come on people! Use common sense. Julia and William lived this life together and sometimes being that down A** B****, things like this happen. I'm sorry for Jennifer's loss but this is all on Julia." – Posted by urbandoesn'tmeanghetto, SunTimes.com

"I don't think you are hard enough on ghetto moms, Mary [Mitchell, the columnist]. You give them a pass, and it is 2008. Racism is dead. Plain and simple. It is long overdue for us to stop paying these people to sit around on the porch, stop giving them free groceries (link cards) stop giving them free money for day care.We have created a mess. And, unfortunately, we do not have the guts to clean it up." – Posted by stroger'sghost, SunTimes.com

The subject of domestic violence frequently draws out the vicious commenters online:

"Why is it that every time I read something in the paper about a boyfirend or husband beating the snot out of his woman, invaribaly it turns out be a black guy...will some enlightened social worker please explain that to me???" – Posted by AniDaati, People.com

According to the Feminist Majority Foundation, an organization dedicated to women's equality, reproductive health, and nonviolence founded in 1987, African-American women experience more domestic violence than do white women between the ages of 20 and 24. A reality is that both black and white women experience the same level of victimization in all other age categories.

Brooklyn Borough President Adams blamed the media for the racism in Internet comments. "When people who make editorial decisions that are not reflective of the city, state, or country at large, they don't have anybody in the room to give a true balance on how we should either be correctly reported on or to make sure that we are not overly reported on," he said. "I find that in the media industry, that the goal when it comes to a white is to merely report the facts there are and move on. But when it comes to a black, particularly a public figure, you don't want to only report the facts; you want to do all you can to destroy that person.

"Young Chris Brown assaulted his lady friend [Rihanna]. He probably would never cut another record," Adams continued. "Charlie Sheen has abused his wife repeatedly. Yet no one has called for him to be banned from movies."

The borough president said whites get a "forgive and forget pass" that blacks do not. "It's not that we should be lax on domestic abuse or criminal behavior, but we should be consistent," Adams said. "That's the key — consistency, not a lax posture."

Just giving birth also seems to make black women the subject of hostile comments.

The controversial and rare octuplet births through in vitro fertilization on Jan. 9, 2009, to Nadya Suleman, a single, then unemployed, divorced white woman from California, eventually drew negative comments from readers. Some readers berated the woman, who already had six other children, and accused her of having mental illness, being irresponsible, and being a burden on taxpayers. In her downward spiral, she tried celebrity boxing and porn to support her children.

Still, those comments were not nearly so bitter and angry as the ones from the Associated Press/AOL story "Michigan Twins Born in Different Years," Jan. 5, 2009, about the black Rochester, Michigan, married mother who gave birth in a rare occurrence to twin boys on two separate days in two separate months and years (Dec. 31, 2008, and Jan. 1, 2009).

Numerous news outlets picked up the story about Tangernika Woods and her husband, Tarrance Griffin Sr. Readers ignored the fact that this couple was legally married with an active father in the home. The overall slant to the comments was that the birth of two black children — regardless of the circumstance — is nothing to celebrate.

"Oh this is so wonderful…let's celebrate two more crack heads born out of wedlock and paid for by taxes of hard working white people…JOY…JOY…AOL ..can you find something good to headline…like…hey two white babies were born of parents that had jobs and it didn't cost tax payers a friggen penny ! when you push bastards out like turds…hey that's wonderful…and you set all kind of records…AOL …good job …as usual." – Posted by wicked98, news.aol.com

Responses to the story were so bad that out of desperation one reader, apparently black, voiced their anger with this:

"The abundant racism on aol.com is appalling. Who is moderating these disgusting, idiotic comments? To those of you who believe that all African-Americans steal, do drugs, and kill people, please get medical attention and step outside of your local McDonald's and back into the real world. Disgusting, disgusting comments." – Posted by Allefra25, news.aol.com

Someone retorted:

"Once again I'm just stating facts, since black people are a minority, statistics can be viewed wrong. The percentage of black children on Welfare compared to white kids. Their are a lot more white kids in the U.S., but, when you do it as a percentage of all black kids, There are 3 times as many black children on welfare than the total percentage of white kids. Check the DCF website. This means black children are three times more likely to be on welfare. Once again, no opinions all facts." – Bcab075, news.aol.com

In many comments, statistics about the racial disparities for public assistance — known as welfare, or Temporary Assistance for Needy Families (TANF) — are often used to "prove" that blacks outnumber whites in receiving the aid.

As of 2010, figures from the U.S. Department of Health and Human Services Administration for Children and Families show that the percentages of white and black welfare recipients, including adults and children, are closer than most think.

According to "Characteristics and Financial Circumstances of TANF Recipients, Fiscal Year 2010," the percentage of African-American TANF Families has slowly decreased since 2001. In 2010, 31.9 percent of families receiving TANF assistance were black or African-American, while 31.8 percent of families receiving the aid were white.

"We are from a 'sound bite' culture, with people who get their culture from television," said anthropologist Sabiyha Prince. "What they see are negative images of regular, working, black people. Somehow, they don't get the same respect. They have visions of welfare mothers, men in jail, etc. I don't know whether to feel sorry for them or disregard them."

On March 20, 2014, Shanesha Taylor, who is black, left two of her children, ages six months and 2 years, in her car while she went on a job interview at an insurance agency in Scottsdale, Arizona. Her third child was in school. After the interview, Taylor came outside and found her car surrounded by cops. She was arrested and jailed for 10 days on two counts of felony child abuse. She also lost custody of her children.

In that instant, Taylor became the poster woman for poverty and single motherhood.

In a June 21, 2014, interview, Taylor told The New York Times that she did not have anywhere else to take her children because the babysitter she had arranged for in advance did not answer the door when she went to drop them off, so she took them with her and left them in the car while she interviewed.

"I felt like this was my opportunity to basically improve life for all of us, and the one key part of it is now not available, so what do I do now?" she said.

In an act of extreme kindness, strangers paid her $9,000 bail through crowdfunding. She received $114,825 in donations in all. In a campaign to get the Maricopa County prosecutor to drop the charges in the case, a Change.org petition generated more than 57,000 signatures. The request was initially refused, but later granted by a judge who required her to deposit $60,000 of the donations into a trust fund for the children's education and care as a condition of her release from jail in July 2014. She also had to attend parenting classes or the original criminal charges would be reinstated. Taylor agreed to the terms. She eventually regained custody of her children, rented a three-bedroom house, and paid for child care.

Amanda Bishop, a young woman from New Jersey, started the online fundraiser for Taylor through a site called youcaring.com. The single mother's story generated so much interest that her fundraiser page attracted 3,603 comments. Many of those included messages of support, but a great number of comments by whites and blacks were very, very angry. Some said that she was being "rewarded" for bad behavior and that other people deserved the money more.

Some others dissected her story, refuting whether she was ever homeless. One of the worst critics was "Terry Berkeley" of Manchester, England, who had seen Taylor's appearance on a British television show and posted a misogynistic rant:

"This stupid irresponsible bitch shouldn't have just been thrown into jail and had her kids taken off her, she should have had her fucking womb cut out too so she can never breed again....People like this are exactly the type of people who should NEVER be allowed breed AT ALL…And there's even an online fundraising page to help this irresponsible bitch???" WHAT???" "Set up by a "woman" surprise, surprise, probably some stupid feminists/women's lib do-gooder making excuses for this deadbeat mother because shes another woman and therefore the world owes her something…Perhaps it was the menopause, PMT, time of the month, or hormones the usual bullshit excuses made for women that made this daft bitch leave her kids on they're own for so long!" The stupid cow was even on Good Morning Britain (previously Daybreak) in the UK this week saying she's do it again. So a job interview is more important than her own kids…Stupid fucking bitch. CUT HER FUCKING WOMB OUT NOW!!" People like her should NEVER, EVER be allowed to breed and while we continue to allow inadequate bitches like this to pro-create society will always be fucked up!!" If you can't afford to have kids THEN DON'T FUCKING HAVE THEM AT ALL…BREED OUT THE INADEQUATES I SAY." – Posted by Terry Berkeley, Shena Simon College, youcaring.com

By any stretch of the imagination, the idea of tearing out of a woman's womb, as described by this poster, is a horrible thought. While most readers agreed that the decision to leave her children in a hot car wasn't the best one, many upheld the very human belief that everyone deserves a second chance.

Unfortunately for Taylor, the original charges for child abuse were reinstated after she reneged on her agreement to deposit $60,000 from the online fundraiser into a bank account for her children. She appeared in court with her pro bono attorney to request to pay less into the fund for the children because she still did not have a job.

Since then, negative follow-up stories about Taylor have dominated the headlines. "Don't let Shanesha's betrayal hurt legit charities," from the editorial board of the Arizona Republic, on azcentral.com on Nov. 3, 2014, implored the public not to be afraid to give to charities during the holidays.

"It's important to stop seeing her as a symbol," the editorial said. "Poverty is widespread in our state. Being poor does not equate with being a scam artist. Taylor is an individual who has made bad choices. Her story shows why it's better to help the poor through donations to well-established charities that have a track record."

Bishop, the organizer of the fundraiser, was interviewed for a story, "Organizer of Shanesha Taylor Fundraiser 'Disappointed,'" published Nov. 8, 2014, on azfamily.com. She said, "A lot of people are saying, 'You must feel stupid, you must feel embarrassed,' and the best way I can put it — I'm not going to feel embarrassed or stupid no matter how this turns out because I know I did something out of the kindness of my heart, and I know everybody who donated did as well." The fundraiser did say, however, that she was upset that Taylor had "agreed to the judge's terms and then backed out."

What most people don't understand is that with crowdfunding, the person who organizes the campaign has nothing to do with receiving or managing the funds after it meets the goal. After the company that manages the transaction takes its percentage ($10,000 in Taylor's case, Bishop said), the recipient is free to do what her or she wants with the funds.

Unfortunately, continuing follow-up stories, including The Huffington Post's "Teary Mom Facing Jail Time Allegedly Spent Donations on 'Baby Daddy's Rap Album,'" published on Nov. 18, 2014, said she spent the money on "trivial things," including studio time so her children's father could record a rap CD.

What doesn't help now is the perception that black single mothers are all scam artists, because people may be more reluctant to help African-American women in dire need. Said Bishop: "We handed her the rope to pull herself out of the hole. The fact that she chose to hang herself with it is beyond our control."

We may never know why Taylor chose not to follow the orders of the court to put some of the money in a trust for her children, or why she chose to spend reportedly $6,000 in recording studio time for her children's father. Actually, it's none of our business. This is something she will have to pay the consequences for, without any of our judgment. Does it mean that she still can't turn her life around? No, it does not.

In a sniper spree spread over three weeks in October 2002, John Allen Muhammad and Lee Boyd Malvo, then age 17, randomly killed 10 people and critically wounded three others in the Washington, D.C., metropolitan area while driving a blue 1990 Chevrolet Caprice sedan. In October 2009, Mildred Muhammad, the former wife of Muhammad, released her memoir, "Scared Silent" (Strebor Books). Her ex-husband was executed by lethal injection one month later. She probably intended the book to be a catharsis after all that her children and she had experienced. In the article "Scared Silent: My Life With the D.C. Sniper," published Oct. 12, 2009, on Lemondrop.com, Muhammad said that she endured mental and emotional abuse by the former Gulf War Veteran. After she divorced him, he kidnapped their children in revenge. Instead of being sympathetic to her after the book release, many readers of the story turned their anger at what he did onto her.

> "Let her go on a book signing and have someone pick her off at 500 meters, that would be justice, she knew what was going on and now is trying to make money off of it, they should pick off her greed driven agent as well as for allowing her to publish her book of excuses, perhaps someone from the families who got killed should set up the shot so she never knows it is coming." – Posted by ROBBERThOEKSTRANNeutral, lemondrop.aol.com

Obviously, "ROBBERThOEKSTRANNeutral" had not had time to read the book, nor was he likely to, so he could not have known whether it was full of "excuses" or not.

Of course, women who choose men who are already convicts for mates will always be an easy target for the online commenters.

Sheila Rule, a retired New York Times journalist, is on a mission to fight against stigmatization, criminalization, and marginalization of both male and female convicts. Eight years ago, she met Joseph Robinson via letters as part of the prison ministry at her church and eventually married him. Together, they formed the "Think Outside the Cell Foundation," which seeks to end the stigma of incarceration and help those who have been in prison to create their own opportunities. Rule wrote in her April 11, 2013, Essence.com piece, "Life After Prison: Battling the Stigma," that people have wanted to know why she would marry a man who had been in prison.

More than 20 years ago, Joseph Robinson was convicted of first-degree murder and is serving a 25-years-to-life sentence. According to his 2008 interview on blogtalkradio.com with Kermit Eady, Robinson got into an altercation with a man who mistakenly thought he had tried to rob him a few months prior in a bar in Utica, New York. As it turned out, another man from East New York, where Robinson is also from, had tried to rob the man in the bar. Because both were from the same neighborhood, the victim assumed both were involved.

At the time, Robinson had been sporadically attending college but also dealing in the drug trade, and he was carrying a weapon. He told Eady that he later encountered the same man who accused him of trying to rob him. They had a confrontation. Robinson said he panicked and shot the man. That was in October 1991. He is still a prisoner at the Sullivan Correctional Facility in Fallsburg, New York, and will be eligible for release in 2017.

"I didn't marry a convict, an inmate, an offender," Rule explained. "I married Joe, and he is all that I've ever hoped for in a husband. Those who do write negative comments about black men rarely consider that a person can truly be rehabilitated after years of confinement."

Rule is not concerned about what others think. She is captivated by her mate. "He's always striving to give his best, to be his best," Rule said of her husband. "He has a sense of purpose and duty: He works to give back to the community he once helped to degrade. With his own boundless potential, he seeks ways to honor the potential of the man whose life he took more than 20 years ago."

Their love story was one of the catalysts for their organization's multimedia documentary, "The Long Shadow of Incarceration's Stigma." The film highlights the plight of formerly incarcerated persons and follows their reentry into society. This issue affects families all over the United States.

On the Essence.com website, which predominately has black readers, comments appeared to be slightly tamer than those on some news websites. A few comments were supportive and agreeable to the point that Rule was making. Others discussed the quandary of being an ex-convict trying to survive post-prison, cases of false imprisonment, and other disparities. The comment from "Balling and tired of the BS" said: "women are quick to marry men outta prison quicker than a man will marry a woman outta prison."

"1Val" responded, "It speaks to the desperation of women befriending and marrying criminals."

Phaedra Parks, an entertainment lawyer, businesswoman, and cast member of the Bravo cable reality television show "The Real Housewives of Atlanta," married Apollo Nida in 2009. At the time, he had already served five years in federal prison for auto title fraud. Parks and Nida have two children together.

According to a CNN story, "'Real Housewives of Atlanta' husband Apollo Nida gets prison for fraud," published on July 9, 2014, Nida was again convicted, this time for bank fraud, identity theft, and other crimes.

U.S. Secret Service Special Agent Alexandre Herrera, interviewed for the article, said in a sworn affidavit that Nida "knowingly and willfully (did) execute and attempt to execute a scheme to defraud federally insured institutions by depositing stolen and fraudulently obtained checks and fraudulently obtained loan proceeds into bank accounts opened in the stolen identities of real persons, and conspire with others to do so, and knowingly convert to his use and the use of others stolen and fraudulently obtained United States Treasury Checks."

Parks found herself on the receiving end of judgmental comments from readers in various online media forums, even after she publicly claimed that she was unaware of her husband's criminal activity. This one came in reaction to a people.com article, "Convicted Real Housewives of Atlanta Star Apollo Nida Slams Wife Phaedra," on July 19, 2014:

> "I've watched her for years. She had made many references to the fact that she had a serious pre-nup. Phaedra is not stupid when it comes to money. She made sure their money was separate, and that they filed taxes separately. I guarantee you that she is going to be able to prove that she not only didn't have any knowledge of the wrong doing, but also that she did not benefit from "his" money in anyway. Phaedra knew what he was from the beginning. I believe that's what she was attracted to. Phaedra has a serious wild streak in her. The "Bad Girl" "Preacher's Kid" with something to prove. She picked him because he was a wild child. I feel she wanted the excitement that came from it, and she enjoyed the feeling of, I'm better than you. I do feel sorry for her children. All the money in the world can not make up for a Mother that is attracted to no good men, and a father that is too selfish and ignorant to put them first either." – Posted by Fat Blond, People.com

The blow-by-blow details of Parks and Nida's troubles aired in Season 7 of the reality series. She did not show up at his sentencing hearing, where he earned eight years for his federal crimes. He asked her for a divorce, and she launched a public relations blitz to tell her part of the story.

In an interview on "The Ellen DeGeneres Show" in October 2014, Parks said she "had no clue that her estranged husband had been engaging in illegal activities" and that she was "blindsided up until the moment he contacted her for help after he was in police custody."

When pressed about why she got involved with an ex-convict, Parks told DeGeneres that when they met in 2009, she was ready to accept his past. She said, "Well, to be honest, he had been to prison. But he was a changed person, so the person I married, I thought had changed."

Most readers of stories about the television appearance did not seem to believe that Parks did not know what her estranged husband was up to. They also brand her as a generally phony person who couldn't possibly be a successful lawyer, based on her decisions. This one was on the gossip website tamaratattles.com:

"Tamara, I cannot believe that this woman is actually sitting on national television claiming she did not know what her husband was up to. Are you kidding me? She knew exactly what he was up to. This fool never had a legitimate job a day in his life. You can best believe that the Feds are crawling up her backside with a microscope. Her tail is in deep trouble. The Feds are not going to let her escape from this. She has the audacity to call herself an attorney. I would not trust her judgement at all. Her record is extremely spotty. BEWARE POTENTIAL CLIENTS!!!" – Posted by Alicia, tamaratattles.com

Shows like the "The Real Housewives of Atlanta" give a distorted view of successful black women, and ratings increase when stereotypical behaviors are on display.

The shows put a spotlight on the people that fit the stereotypes and ignore those who don't, said Monnica Williams, the clinical psychologist. "With black women, you can't win either way, and that's the definition of oppression — when you don't have any good choices."

"If you put 'black women' in Google images, what comes up is usually horrific," Williams said. "They're sexualized objects or the opposite, the stereotype of the angry black woman, the large, unattractive, really nasty domineering one. We have these subtypes of African-American women that, again, fit right into these pathological stereotypes, and basically society in a sense will reward black women who fit into these stereotypes because that's what they expect. And the ones who don't are punished in many ways."

Welfare mothers and convicts' wives aside, Michelle Obama is a triple-educated wife, a mother, *and* a lawyer. She is part of the successful nuclear family model to which most of us aspire, and the product of such a family, yet she still cannot be free of coarse stereotypes. She would not likely receive the cover line "National Treasure — Grown-Ass Woman!" like white singer Taylor Swift did for the cover of Elle Magazine's June 2015 issue. Even though she is America's first African-American first lady, her accomplishments are not enough.

Sophia A. Nelson's story "Black. Female. Accomplished. Attacked," July 20, 2008, from The Washington Post, discusses the racist double standard that educated, professional, and prominent black women have to face. She wrote about how during the 100th anniversary celebration of her sorority, Alpha Kappa Alpha, many of her peers discussed the "mischaracterization" of Michelle Obama during Barack Obama's first presidential campaign.

Nelson wrote: "We've watched with a mixture of pride and trepidation as the wife of the first serious African-American presidential contender has weathered recent campaign travails — being called unpatriotic for a single offhand remark, dubbed a black radical because of something she wrote more than 20 years ago and plastered with the crowning stereotype: 'angry black woman.' And then being forced to undergo a politically mandated 'makeover' to soften her image and make her more palatable to mainstream America."

Nelson, who is also a lawyer, received several strong tongue-lashings from readers who supposed that her reason (and those of other black writers) for doing the story was to "suck up" to the Obamas.

"Hey, Ms. Nelson--Michelle Obama may not tote a gun, but she is angry, she is derogatory about the United States, and she reeks of a sense of entitlement. I don't like her, I don't like her sista-mouth, I don't want her as first lady, and if I were close to voting for Barack Obama (which I am not), the fact that he is married to that woman would be enough to assure that I didn't. And guess what, Ms. Nelson: I don't dislike blacks, I don't dislike "powerful women", I just dislike Michelle. But, you really out to cool off, because the Obamas will not be occupying the White House any time soon." – Posted by TimeforChange, WashingtonPost.com

In comments about the first lady, nearly every inch of her has been scrutinzed — her hairstyles, her facial features, her complexion, the shape of her arms, the size of her behind, her weight — things that most people would be mortified to have discussed in the public square.

"Michelle Obama's posterior again the subject of a public rant," a Washington Post story, received 7,974 comments. Reader "dstiebs" responded saying: "I also belive Michelle Obama does have a fat butt. I also don't like what queers do because it does go against God and Jesus's teachings. Of course I won't get fired or suspended for my comments but the paper won't publish my remarks either."

Then there was this one from "walkman321," who said: "If there was a place for a 'caution wide load" sign that would be her. Wonder if she takes two seats on an airplane."

I do not recall criticism of any other first lady's rear end, and mentioning it automatically sexualizes her in a way that is not flattering, but that is nothing new. Some readers who comment also accuse her of actually being a man and compare her to apes. Those types of stories simply open her up to more condemnation online, voicing the notion that Michelle Obama is not a "proper" first lady.

In the story "Michelle Obama 'Doesn't' Look Or Act' Like A First Lady, Says Virginia Voter Bobbie Lussier," published in The Huffington Post on Sept. 28, 2012, the voter from Virginia, who was interviewed at an American Legion meeting in Indianapolis, gave NPR's Ari Shapiro her opinion of the president and his wife: "I just — I don't like him. Can't stand to look at him. I don't like his wife. She's far from the first lady. It's about time we get a first lady in there that acts like a first lady and looks like a first lady."

Reader "Polly McDonald" wrote this comment in response to the article: "There's nothing Presidential about Obama, and there's nothing

First Ladylike about his wife. Race has got nothing to do with it. They're casual in dress and in word, and that's a direct reflection of how seriously they take their positions."

Some people use any excuse to tear down the Obamas, because while they can embrace the technology that allows them to scrutinize their every move, they don't seem to understand that we are living in 2015, not the 1800s.

Readers use comments to tear apart Michelle Obama's every word, letter by letter, in order to continue their online evisceration of her. This reader of a syracuse.com story, "Critics lash out at Michelle Obama's Tuskegee University Speech (What they're saying)," published May 13, 2015, could not stick to the point of the story with this response:

"It is obvious that Michelle is prejudiced against European-Americans even though she herself has European genetics and is married to a biracial man. Besides, if she is so proud to be of African descent only, why does she have her hair "straightened"?" – Posted by capwasteh20, Syracuse.com

Readers act as though, because she is the first lady, somehow any previous experiences with racism must be removed from her record because she is supposedly proof that we are living in a post-racial society.

This comment is typical of many readers who accuse her of being racist and un-American.

"I hope Michelle is being a cynical, political hack, rather than believing her racialist nonsense. Blacks with the same education experience as whites earn the same $. Blacks who marry successfully, like ALL demographics, have a less than 10% of remaining in poverty. You drop single motherhood, and poverty rates look very different. Illegitimacy rates in Baltimore and other big cities is 70%+. This would impoverish and destroy ANY demographic, and does. Democrats. Michelle and her husband get no political mileage talking about that reality, which would undermine most of her speech. And what a message for the young grads - this is a racist nation and you will have untold burdens, in 2015? BS" – Posted by pajes, Syracuse.com

One topic that should be completely off-limits should be the Obama's lovely daughters, Malia and Sasha, who are now teenagers. Unfortunately, commenters consider them fair game to be criticized as harshly as their parents in everything from their hairstyles to their clothing choices. Political pundits have even suggested that the girls needed to act more "classy."

In January 2009, the first lady criticized Ty Inc., the maker of Beanie Babies, for naming their two new dolls "Sweet Sasha" and "Marvelous Malia," the names of her daughters, who were ages 7 and 10 at the time. She received the gamut of negative comments about her criticism of the use of her children's names.

Through a White House spokesperson, she said: "We believe it is inappropriate to use young, private citizens for marketing purposes." Although the company claimed that the dolls were not inspired by the "first daughters," the toys were "retired" and renamed in Ferbruary 2009.

Many news outlets carried versions of the story of her reaction to the toys, and comments mostly took on a "How dare she?" tone, instead of commiseration for a parent wanting a level of privacy for her minor children.

Responders to the Associated Press story "Sasha and Malia Dolls Miff First Lady," published Jan. 25, 2009, were more than excited to use the section to castigate the entire family. However, this rant just goes far beyond where any idea of freedom of speech should go:

"Come on Michelle put on your designer big girl panties and suck it up like you really are a for the first time in your life proud to be an American. Back in the day the best black children could hope for a far as national commercial recognition went was Tar Baby licorice candy. ===your little baseard can look forward to being a porn star, a d**k in the azz, a d**K in the pu**y, a d**k in the mouth, all at once, go hillbilly sue." – Posted by CShae89546, news.aol.com

Readers seemed also not to appreciate her rights as a parent to criticize the marketing of the dolls with these:

"WHO GIVES A SHIT WHAT MOZILLA THINKS ABOUT ANYTHING SHES A BIG OL DOG WITH KINKEY HAIR,,,, LIKE TO SEE HER WITH HAIR NORMAL ,, NOT IRONED STRAIGHT HER CHOICE OF COLOR OF CLOTHES IS [TIPICAL] SUPERBAD." – Posted by Sam b tree, news.aol.com

Another reader said:

"Hmmm, so Michelle's "miffed", eh? Who knew that the Obamas have a copyright on the names "Sasha" and "Malia". You're in the limelight now folks, this is what you signed up for . . . get used to it. The American people paid $650,000,000 for the Obama package . . . they are entitled to their money's worth any way they want it." – Posted by Justmyopinion999, news.aol.com

Still another one said:

"These people are the racist ones!! Nothing would have been said about white dolls. So why is it an issue. Barbie came out with black dolls did not see anyone getting mad about that. So I hope you really think about the fact that racism goes 2 ways." – Posted by Windypalm, news.aol.com

I would love to know what the first lady thinks of comments written about her, but I doubt that reading them is high on her agenda. The best part about Michelle Obama is that she doesn't have to back down on her beliefs to please a society that refuses to accept her and her family. She is a strong black woman in every sense of the word — academically and physically — with no stereotypes attached.

CHAPTER 5

Equal Education

"As every empirical study of Intelligence affirms what has come to be known as the racial Hierarchy of IQ, Asians on top, Whites in the middle and Blacks and certain Latino ethnicities on the bottom, it is perfectly natural that those students displaying the competencies required for admittance to Gifted Learning curriculum should reflect that Racial Hierarchy of Intelligence." – Posted by Jacob handelsman, surfzupp@cox.net, NYTimes.com, June 19, 2008

IT HAS BEEN 60 YEARS since the 1954 Brown vs. Board of Education landmark Supreme Court case, which overturned racial segregation in public schools on the grounds that "separate educational facilities are inherently unequal." Fast forward to contemporary times and see that readers often disparage the intelligence and behaviors of black students. Negative comments often accompany stories that may offer a glimmer of hope that the public educational system in need of repair on a national level can be fixed.

Predominantly black neighborhoods, even ones in suburban areas like those on Long Island, rarely have surplus monies, and their schools are often underperforming. Yet when the predominantly black Long Island school district of Roosevelt found itself with a surplus $9 million to spend on student services, some readers appeared to think that blacks weren't worth the funding. They took it to the next level when responding to the May 2008 Newsday.com story "Roosevelt: $9M More for Schools."

"I also know that **** have had their hands out since the white folks took the guilt trip. Government handouts to fatherless youngsters is not the way to go. Time to stop it. Naturally low IQ's with a high testosterone level is a very dangerous combination." – Posted by Spunky, Uniondale, N.Y., Newsday.com

When African-Americans or other minorities are on the receiving end of funding, readers seem to equate it to "handouts" or "entitlements," something that President Obama continues to be accused of offering in his second term. Many of the online critics opine that he won the black vote because African-Americans are dependent on government handouts. The haters are also quick to jump to the conclusion that *all* the children in the district are fatherless, dumb, and welfare-dependent. Even in the suburbs, the racists assume, black children cannot have high IQs and two hard-working parents who paid taxes, too.

"A 23% increase in spending? Someone is paying for it, in this case other NYers. Why should other Nyers' subsidize Roosevelt? When someone is giving you the money and you don't have to work of it as is the case in most Black 'Communities' you don't care how it gets spent as long as you get 'yours'. Same old same old in Roosevelt. They will be looking for another 'one time bailout' in a couple of years. And they will get it because Whites don't want to be accused of being insensitive Racists. Maybe People should wake up to see who the real Racists are. They run Roosevelt." – Posted by ExNewYorker, Newsday.com

The commenter has erroneously identified the school's surplus as a "bailout" simply because the money would be going to a largely black community. Government bailouts or financial support are given out only in emergencies, generally to help a company or country avoid bankruptcy.

A Dec. 22, 2008, New York Daily News story, "Teacher ripped class with N-word, say students," reported that some black students accused their white teacher at a middle school in Park Slope, a Brooklyn neighborhood, of using the racial slur while teaching. According to news reports, she scolded the class using the word after some students became disruptive while watching a film. Although teacher Elvira Sacco denied using the slur, some readers who responded to the article said the teacher had made a "faux pas." Yet others were sympathetic to the educator's exasperation and argued that she had reached her breaking point at a school where 90 percent of the students were black and Hispanic. It is baffling to understand how she thought using a racial epithet would motivate the students to behave more appropriately.

One comment suggested the N-word was no worse than other racial slurs and raised the frequently heard defense that the N-word was acceptable since some blacks use it regularly among themselves:

> "W op, G uinea, G reasball, G oombah, D ago, These are just words.All raceshave them.None are worse than others, Yes, not even the N-word.Stop thinking your special and have Carte Blanch on the derogatory words.I hear blacks ABUSE this word daily.I saw Kat Williams on HBO,,if this word was not invented ,,,it would be hard to sell his show based on one or two words besides N*****, that he so fondly uses! "man, whats up with N****** now a days?, M***** F***in N******.My main N***** is a N*****, Dis N***** went to Dis one store that a n***** owned, Dis N***** told dis one N***** that some N***** just robbed his N*****a**" And as the camera panned the crowd, EVERY single black person was laughing their b utts off ! BUT,,,,,,,,,wrong word to use in a class room full of children,,,I wonder if it would be acceptable if Kat was a teacher???????????" – Posted by Broccoli Rob, NYDailynews.com

The next year, the Board of Education (BOE) found after an investigation that the teacher had in fact used the racial epithet. According to a Gothamist.com story in May 2009, a student who witnessed the teacher's outburst and later transferred to another school told BOE investigators that she said, "You don't know how to act. You're acting lower class. You're acting like a whole bunch of n-----."

The teacher was reassigned, pending disciplinary action from the BOE.

The comment above was similar to many replies to the story about the teacher that suggested that the students should not have been offended if they were not acting like "niggers."

> "It does sound like these "kids" were disrupting the movie and behaving low class. Everybody KNOWS that black people talk to the movie screen! How you gonna believe a 14-year-old named 'Tyasia'! This white teacher should give up trying to teach these black kids, and move to the suburbs. Anyway, what's the big deal? Young black people use the N word with each other all the time; ever walk behind black kids in downtown Brooklyn? They love it!" – Posted by footstool, NYDailynews.com

One commenter even claimed that the teacher was simply calling them "ignorant," swearing that the term was the actual definition of "nigger" and that she was using the word correctly. It begs the question: Apart from hip-hop references, why is it that the word "nigger" applies to African-Americans who have behaved badly?

In Merriam-Webster's online dictionary, the current definition describes the term as *"usually offensive; see usage paragraph below*: a black person" and *"usually offensive; see usage paragraph below*: a member of any dark-skinned race." In reader comments about the definition on the website, posters debated each other over their own ideas of what they thought it meant, using the words "disadvantaged person of any race, "and "low integrity, no standards, full of corruption and dishonest." It is doubtful that any European member of organized crime has ever been referred to as a nigger.

"People need to get a grip and learn that words cannot hurt you… if you are not a n-word then it cannot hurt you. Period.. I'm not 'white trash' and I have never been called white trash. Why? Because I don't act like white trash…sometimes if the name fits you have to wear it…life is tough. If you don't like it change." – Posted by commonsense1971, NYDailynews.com

These stories are in a long line of others that fueled intense debate over the use of the N-word, over who "owns" the right to say or use it. Some of the comments on articles in the case have hammered home the idea that a double standard applied to the use of the word, as in when white people ask, "If black people can use it, why can't white people?"

White people also seem to have taken as fact that the word is used as a "term of endearment" among blacks. In fact, it has different meanings when black people say it, and it can have connotations that are quite de-rogatory when used against another black person.

Chuck D, the Public Enemy rapper, says it depends on the context: "As far as black folks are concerned, it's always been 'pool room' language and the back corners of the street language. It was never meant to be brought out to the forefront as this hip slang."

The rapper's explanation for "why people chime in with the stereo-type that we call ourselves the 'N-word'" is complicated.

"A lot of our stuff that used to be behind closed doors, or on the dark end of the street, now is brought into mainstream forefront and is used as an excuse that anybody can say it because it's a part of our culture," he said. "But somebody else will have to say it's full of crap, too, and we don't have enough of that.

"We have to ask: 'Who came up with that?'" he continued. "Nobody seems to address people when they should be, like, 'Well, who told you that? How did you come up with this, and who gave you the audacity to come up with that?' Nobody ever seems to come up with an answer when they are challenged. They say, 'Well, you know, this is what people do.'

[Ask them] 'Who? Who?' Then there is a lot of stuttering when they're confronted on their point of view with something of substance."

Reader comments in the New York Daily News online after the Board of Education's decision in 2009 boldly implied that black children were a lost cause because of an African-American "tradition" of poor parenting.

"What else would you call these animal monkeys?? They are taught by their parents from birth to no take orders from any-one...especially white authoritative figures!" – Posted by Vinny, NYDailynews.com

The 2001 "No Child Left Behind Act" has, for the most part, attempted to raise the bar on underperforming schools, low test scores, and graduation rates. According to a New York Daily News analysis, a disproportionate number of black and Latino students are stuck in that city's worst schools. Adding insult to injury are comments by readers about stories that focus on issues plaguing public schools, such as a lack of resources or availability of qualified teachers. These comments generally trumpet a false truth that black children do not want to learn.

"We are not teaching them what they need to live the way they want to live, i.e., why would a negro want to learn grammar, or how to read, or adding and subtracting? What does that have to do with 'chillin', or 'rappin' or just hanging around? Teach them African History, Ebonics, and basket weaving so at least they know their roots...how about the art of Lion Hunting? Or Spear Chucking? How about 'The Art of Monkey'...ah, what's the use; save the money and teach the kids who want to get ahead, etc., but now we have a new president and everything will 'change' now. God save the Republicans." – Posted by ChuckSherwin, NYDailynews.com

In 2009, Joel I. Klein, then chancellor of New York City public schools, and the Rev. Al Sharpton wrote a letter in The Wall Street Journal to newly elected President Obama saying that America was facing its "last great civil-rights battle:" the racial education gap. They also pointed out that the "average 12th-grade black or Hispanic student has the reading, writing, and math skills of an eighth-grade white student." They had created the nonpartisan "Education Equality Project" the previous year, asking the president to develop national standards and assessments for student achievement. They noted that students who graduate from urban high schools still are unprepared for college and gainful employment, and urged him to redirect federal funds to support the recruitment and retention of some of the best teachers in underserved urban schools.

Other news websites picked up the story and comments about the Klein-Sharpton initiative. In this exchange between two commenters, it was apparent that the blame is on black parents, cast as making excuses for their children's education:

"What about parents, parents, parents?" – Posted by Artiss999, newser.com

"Oh no, it's not EVER the parents fault..it's all the schools and the white people, I can't count how many times in school I have seen ENGLISH 1301 WHITE VERSION, BLACK VERSION, CHINESE VERSION, HISPANIC VERSION, Ect.......if all the books are the same for everybody at the very begining, and remain so throughout the entire curriculum then the big difference is????....MY daughter is a straight A student, why because she is white?.....NO...because I work my butt off to support my family, so my wife can spend the time needed to (just an expression folks...not literally) beat the education into my daughter....Parents raising their kids is where it starts....Poor decisions return poor results......I chose not to do drugs, not to drink excessively, and did 4 years in the NAVY, and they payed for my education when

I got out, and thats how I got started, by good decisions......My daddy wasn't rich either, so any excuse about *well we aint rich like yall * isbullsh**....first and foremost, it's the parents...a mother of 5 welfare crack smoking parent will not likely have children that grow up to be doctorsand lawers...A single parent of 5 or more that strives to keep themself clean and works hard to get their kids educated, and takes charge of the familly, and not claim victim status, on the otherhand may have good results." – Posted by riffriffran, newswer.com

Just one year after The Wall Street Journal letter, a New York Times article, "'No Child' Law Is Not Closing a Racial Gap," on April 28, 2009, illuminated the same old troubles for black and Hispanic students.

Freeman Hrabowski III, president of the University of Maryland, Baltimore, who was interviewed in the story, said, "Where we see the gap narrowing, that's because there's been an emphasis on supplemental education, on after-school programs that encourage students to read more and do more math problems. Where there are programs that encourage additional work, students of color do the work and their performance improves and the gap narrows."

Hrabwoski, co-writer of "Beating the Odds: Raising Academically Successful African American Males," Oxford University Press, 1998, said that educators and middle-class parents who are encouraging stronger educational achievement, are competing against popular culture that says "it's simply not cool for students to be smart."

Almost any education story about minority students draws comparisons among black, Asian, and white students. In comments, people seem to enjoy quoting "bootstrap" stories like this one, of Asian families, while demeaning black students:

"I live in the Bay Area and work in San Francisco. The inner city schools here, both in Oakland and San Francisco, have thousands of poor Asian immigrant kids whose parents often do not speak

English. These kids go to the same school and have the same teachers as the inner city black and Hispanic kids. Amazingly, the Asian kids thrive and succeed, while the black kids usually fail. It all comes down to culture. The Asian parents, supported by their community, insist on excellence in school. They know that's the key to their kids' future success. Sadly, in the black community, there is an avoidance and denigration of academic achievement. The results are clear. Until there is a change in the black community, this cycle of failure will continue," – Posted by Scott, CA, NYTimes.com

Although retorts to this story complained about the teachers and about cultural bias in tests, the nail in the coffin is the ubiquitous belief that black children do not have the desire or aptitude to excel in school.

"... We need to say that which shall not be spoken. By the third grade, the natural course of black school children permanently reflects intellectual inferiority to whites, Asians, and Latinos (language adjusted) in learning skills development and ability. The ills of black culture, beginning from before birth, are largely responsible for this inferior preparation. Argue the source if you will, but this practical inferiority, once established, is intractable and sets a course through life, with dependence upon arbitrary handouts from inept, but politically correct race arbitrators, like those in New Haven..." – Posted by actingwhite, NYTimes.com

Dahlma Llanos Figueroa, an Afro-Latina who is author of "Daughters of the Stone" (St. Martin's Press, 2009), is especially concerned that black people contribute to the negative images that commenters seem to prey on. "I have come to hate the term 'keeping it real' because so many of the people whom I speak with equate that with such negative qualities," she said.

Llanos Figueroa thinks the term should mean for us to present all the facets of our communities, be they flaws, virtues, problems, solutions, failures, and successes.

"We run into problems when we buy into the lie that because we are black, we all have the same life experiences," she adds. "Many comments are aimed at pointing out and exaggerating problems without considering causes or attempts at understanding the problem. They just jump to conclusions based on their limited perceptions and paint all of us with the same brush. The people who are putting it out there are doing it on purpose with the intent to distort, divide, and destroy."

Year after year, new studies specifically related to black students appear in publications that underscore racial disparities. According to the New York Times article "Black Students Face More Discipline, Data Suggests," March 6, 2012, one in five black boys and more than one in 10 black girls received out-of-school suspensions. Overall, black students were three and a half times more likely to be suspended or expelled as their white peers.

Reacting to the report, then-U.S. Secretary of Education Arne Duncan said, "The undeniable truth is that the everyday education experience for too many students of color violates the principle of equity at the heart of the American promise."

Online commenters generally were less sympathetic.

"When there was institutional segregation the out of wedlock birthrate (1964) for Black families was 7%. Negligible for Whites. Now 70% of births to Black women are in single parent families. Seperte but equal (segregation) did not cause the social problems we see today. We have enabled and institutionalized marginalized communities with government support and the cocept of "rights" to the unending financial and medical support of the government. Congratulation Progressive Liberals. When Senator P. Moynihan wrote a book on what would happen he was called a racist. He was right. Change the culture and behavior of the Black community. Before that is done epect nothing to change. NO government policy has been able to change the dynamic because the only thing Liberals want to do is train the people to be community organizers so they can demand more from the productive class. Bad strategy, but the left is unable to open its eyes." – Posted by Ted, Syracuse, New York, NYTimes.com

The number of black students who are held up as negative examples in news articles is very likely a small fraction of the total. Many black students not only learn, but also succeed academically to graduate school and beyond. Many news stories have "good news/bad news" prognoses, even ones meant to be positive about blacks and education. Those usually say that African-Americans are doing better, but essentially intimate that they may never reach the same height of achievement that whites and Asian students do. Some studies suggest otherwise.

In November 2013, the Journal of Blacks in Higher Education reported that black student graduation rates at 13 high-ranking colleges and universities were very close to that of their white peers or higher. Among the good news was that 97 percent of black students at Harvard University earned their degrees in six years. At Amherst College, the number was 94 percent, both Yale University and Swarthmore had 94 percent, while Princeton University and the University of Pennsylvania had 93 percent. The JBHE also documented that at five top women's colleges, the black student graduation rate was actually higher than the rate for white students.

The cyberspace haters who can quote and twist all the negative data never seem to know about these kinds of statistics, or acknowledge the existence of high-achieving black students.

Mark Potok, the editor at the Southern Poverty Law Center, said, "I am not African-American, so I don't pretend to speak for black people, but I mean I would say it can't be pleasant to realize what enormous loathing there is in certain quarters for black people."

"My guess is that most black people understand that at some level, but you know you read these comments and sometimes and your hair stands on end. You go to websites like 'chimpout.com' — it's unreal," he said. "So I don't see how that could be good for a person. What could it be like to be a teenage black kid, a boy or a girl growing up and reading this stuff? I think many young black kids today, if they are not exposed to that, think that the United States is a hell of a better place than it used to be. That's certainly true, but it's not all that great. Nevertheless, that becomes obvious when you look at some of these comments."

CHAPTER 6

Black Men and the Animal Instinct

"It's ridiculous the blame game that goes on in these decrepit communities. These people (young men ages 14-35) are very violent, hypersexual and impulsive which is a lethal combination. They'll kill to save face, kill when angered, kill out of jealousy, kill to quench sexual urges, kill in the commission of a robbery and kill just for sport." – Posted by jabreal100, WashingtonPost.com, May 6, 2008

BLACK MEN UNDERSTAND THAT THEY are among the most vilified people in the world, but to be constantly reminded it of it in the media must be a particularly bitter pill. The Trayvon Martin case ushered in a particularly difficult period to be a black man or to read about black men.

"Trayvon Martin was killed by George Zimmerman as a public service. Zimmerman knew Trayvon Martin was a dirty ass uncivilized street nigger that needed to be killed." – Posted by LenPeterson, YouTube.com

Nothing in Martin's background or upbringing suggested he was any of those things. In fact, his family told The New York Times that he was a kindhearted, gentle kid who had taken honors classes, was preparing for his SAT, and was interested in aeronautics. He did odd jobs and helped care for relatives. His parents were divorced but both held middle-class jobs and were both involved in his life. Naturally, his alleged misdeeds were thrust into the limelight — school suspensions, marijuana smoking, theft — in order to downplay reaction to the unjustified killing.

A commenter "Great Caesar Obama" to the Feb. 24, 2015, Washingtontimes.com story "George Zimmerman won't face federal charges for Trayvon Martin death: Justice Department" stated in part that the "FACTS as brought out in the trial were: "Trayvon Martin was a drug dealer and burglar who was walking between houses and looking into window when he was spotted by Zimmerman."

Although that story mentioned that Martin seemed suspicious to his killer, there is nothing in the article that states that the young man was a drug dealer or burglar.

In contrast, there were many supporters of George Zimmerman, the man who killed him. The article "Zimmerman supporters afraid to go public; fear backlash over Travon Martin Shooting," from the Associated Press in the New York Daily News on March 28, 2012, painted a different picture of the accused killer who some of his friends and neighbors said was being demonized, while Martin was being portrayed as an "angel."

The idea that black people were upset and wanted to see justice for the young man apparently did not sit too well with this reader who clearly had issues with black women.

"Oh my. Stand for justice? No rush to judgement "profiled, stalked and killed"? Black people, especially black women, wouldn't know what justice meant if it bit you the leg. I don't know if this is a genetic issue having to do with intelligence or extra testosterone or some other black issue. For the record, I am not hispanic or a jew. I dont have any particular reason to support Zimmerman except for the fact that a group of savages seem to want to tear him apart. You folks look compassionless and mad. For the record, white women think black women are mean, blood thirsty and foolish.

You all out did yourselves with this tragic issue. Your deserve all the derision society bestows upon you. Good luck." – Posted by Marieinbethpage, NYDailynews.com

In many comments about African-Americans who experience racism in its many forms, it appears that people think that we are not supposed to get mad about anything. We are not supposed to fight back because, according to their distorted outlook, we cause our own trouble.

In 2013, the Coalition to Stop Gun Violence, a nonprofit group based in Washington, D.C., released a public service announcement (PSA) reenacting the altercation between Martin and Zimmerman and used 911 tapes presented during Zimmerman's trial. An Aug. 20, 2013, article about it, "Anti-stand your ground reenacts Trayvon Martin shooting," published on yahoonews.com logged a whopping 10,695 comments.

I was unable to get through all of them, but many of the earlier responses criticized the PSA, saying that Zimmerman was the victim. Other comments questioned what individuals would do if they were faced with the same dilemma if the stand your ground law went away and why no PSAs were done about other crimes committed against whites by African-Americans. Many of the comments were rants about Martin, a young man the writers had never met.

"Here's a better PSA. Show a negligent mother and father ignoring their children at a young age. Then show the criminal progression as the child develops, first doing illegal drugs, joining a gang, breaking into homes, selling drugs, posting the "thug lifestyle" on FB, then trying to be a badass, and running into the wrong guy protecting his neighborhood." – Posted by spewing venom619, news.yahoo.com

"Trayvon should have never been shot because he should have been in prison for prior issues. His continued living on the criminal side caused his end of life. Better the law violator be dead than some innocent person." – Posted by Robert, news.yahoo.com

In the years since the death of their son, Sybrina Fulton and Tracy Martin have continued to speak to the public about topics that disproportionately affect the civil rights of African-Americans. The bereaved parents lend their support to other parents who have found themselves in the same predicament. In stories about Martin's parents' speaking engagements, readers use comment forums to demean the dead young man and his parents.

Buffalonews.com published the article "Trayvon Martin's father to speak at SUNY Fredonia" on Feb. 5, 2015, about a talk that he was giving about his son during Black History Month. Comments about the event on that State University of New York campus made it seem as though he was making such appearances for the fame and glory, and they took shots at the university for allowing the talk:

> "Parents exploiting their dead thug, gangster kids for money; the new black thing. And the most money is made if the kid is was killed by someone white (just not black) especially a cop."-Posted by BJC, Buffalonews.com

> "His son had a bad attitude and should have walk away from any confrontations. That is here nor there this doesn't build up race relations and is not a positive thing for the university. I think the students would rather have free food to celebrate black history month. But the way, what month is White, Asian, Latino, history month. This is all crap about celebrating American history month." – Posted by aldonco, Buffalonews.com

When Fulton, Martin's mother, spoke at Colorado State University at another Black History Month event about her son's death, she received the same "warm" welcome online that his father did. In "Mother of Trayvon Martin to speak at CSU Thursday," published Feb. 16, 2015, on

Coloradoan.com, a reader, "Jason Joseph, works at Nikon," said: "What will she speak about? How her poor non-existent parenting caused the death of her child. Anything other that that is just made up non-sense."

Another commenter, "Barry Hirsh, Williamsport Area Senior High School," asked: "What gives credence to the mother of a thug who was responsible for his own undoing to speak as an expert on anything?"

As if it wasn't bad enough Martin's parents lost their son in a questionable death, readers who comment seem to think that his parents should walk around with their heads hung in shame and keep quiet. I'm glad they're not doing that. They have every right to speak about it to as many people as they can until *they* are tired of doing so.

It takes a great deal of audacity for Martin and Fulton to speak out in person about a controversial topic that has affected their family. The same cannot be said about online commenters, because it's easier for them to hide behind a computer screen.

Michael Brown also had two parents involved in his life, but that didn't stop the unarmed man from being killed in a controversial shooting by a police officer on Aug. 9, 2014, in Ferguson, Missouri. Although he might have, according to reports after the incident, stolen from a store, it did not mean that he should have been killed for it.

"But in many cases, people have a knee-jerk reaction when it comes to racial issues," NABJ's Butler said. "As if black people don't deserve due process. That kind of stuff really gets to me."

This comment is an example of that:

"I find it insane that black people act like every time they walk out the front door they are dodging police bullets, when the statistics are that 93 % of black murders are caused by black people. Not only that, a kid fights with a cop and gets shot because of it, they don't recognize that the kid still would be alive today if he hadn't fought with a cop! Then they wonder why white people think they are stupid! Amazing" – Posted by Electroguy1 CharleyC, CNN.com

In the aftermath, Brown's death set off a chain of violent protests and marches in Ferguson, resulting in clashes with police in riot gear with tear gas.

Comments for the CNN story "Witnesses to Michael Brown's shooting detail his last minutes" were closed after 2,683 responses. At least one of them complained about CNN's coverage of the shooting and its aftermath with this:

> "If CNN devoted this much attention to the extreme dysfunction in the black underclass, perhaps the black underclass would start taking responsibility for its own dysfunction. Black on black crime: no problem. Black on white crime: no problem. White on black crime: QUELLE HORREUR!!! STOP THE PRESSES!!! LOOT THE 'HOOD!!! So glad that our first post-racial president has had such a medicinal affect on black dysfunction. Next up: the race hustlers." – Posted by ExJAG, CNN.com

Another reader followed up with a sarcastic admonition:

> "Careful because if u speak sensibly black people will call u a racist. And god forbid u tell a black person anything different or they'll attack u and bob their heads with their ghetto attitudes as if we are suppose to far them simply because they're black." – Posted by SfDumb, CNN.com

Some readers justifiably complained about the looting that followed Brown's death, but seemed to imply that other blacks condoned the actions. Yes, the people looting, setting fires, and shooting during the protests did not help the situation, but the behavior was not endorsed by all African-Americans.

> "Everything ive said, aside for a moment. I lost all sympathy and support when the rioting and looting began, especially when I saw the

hundreds of racist black folks tweeting telling people to go loot white homes and businesses. Sorry, I no longer care about Michael Brown. In fact that impacted my opinion of the thing so greatly, id prefer if it was swept under the rug. You people can't act civilized, no justice no peace? How can they conduct an investigation when you people wont stop assaulting innocents, robbing businesses and burning gas stations? You cry for an answer yet you aren't letting them do their jobs. Sooner you go home sooner they can take 90% of the police force off the streets." – Posted by Hurr Durr, CNN.com

The emotions that played out on comment threads on July 17, 2014, were not really much different from others that blame victims for their own misfortunes.

Eric Garner, a 43-year-old married father of six from New York's Staten Island, was killed by a police officer who used an illegal chokehold on him after he resisted arrest when accused of selling loose cigarettes. Garner, who had just broken up a fight outside a store, denied doing anything wrong when the police approached him, and no clear evidence emerged that he actually sold any cigarettes that day.

The man did have a police record, but it was not a reason for him to be killed.

The incident was captured in a video that went viral, watched by millions of people. It showed that Garner told the officers 11 times that he could not breathe while lying face down on the sidewalk. It was further revealed that the rescue workers who came to the scene did not try to save him by administering CPR or other potentially life-saving support because the officers told them that he was breathing on his own. The EMTs did not administer any emergency medical aid nor promptly place him on a stretcher. He was eventually transported to Richmond University Medical Center, but police said he died of a heart attack en route. He was pronounced dead at the hospital one hour later.

During protests and other events surrounding the unarmed man's death, the Rev. Al Sharpton used his National Action Network organization to help Garner's family find justice. According to the medical examiner's findings, Garner's death was "a result of compression of neck (chokehold), compression of the chest and prone positioning during physical restraint by police." That report also said that Garner had asthma and heart disease and was overweight, which were contributing factors. While Garner's medical conditions may have posed health issues for him in the future, the man probably was not going to die on that particular day, at that specific time, from his health conditions. Readers found it much easier to blame him for his own demise in these comments:

"This fat criminal didn't die because of lack of oxygen, he died from a heart attack brought about from the stress of resisting arrest. Had he simply put his hands behind his back and NOT RESISTED arrest he would still be here! He caused this by HIS actions, not the cops and not ems -- but the race- baiter (who never shows up when black thugs shoot each other left and right), will clog the streets and collect the cash." – Posted by Buckster, NYDailynews.com

This reader used stereotyping to make her point:

"Let's be honest, the giant of a man resisted arrest and the NYPD did what they could to subdue him. I saw a choke-hold applied haphazardly for a moment, but if we're still honest here, that's not what he died from. He died from being overly obese and un-healthy." – Posted by Sarah Uno, MSNBC.com

The case against Daniel Pantaleo, the officer who choked Garner, went to a grand jury on Sept. 29, 2014. On Dec. 3, 2014, it was announced that the grand jury would not indict him for Garner's death. He and another officer were reassigned. The Garner family filed a $75 million wrongful death lawsuit against New York City, the NYPD, and six NYPD officers. On July 13, 2015, four days before the first anniversary of Garner's death, his family settled with the City of New York for $5.9 million, which would also prevent any further lawsuits against the city for the death of Eric Garner. In addition, the family settled for an undisclosed amount of money with the Richmond University Medical Center in Staten Island.

Garner's mother, Gwen Carr, who spoke at a press conference about the settlement on July 14, said: "Don't congratulate us. This is not a victory. The victory will come when we get justice."

Readers of an AP article on the incident were unsympathetic:

"Nothing says I love you than profiting handsomely from the tragic death of your morbidly obese petty criminal relative. It is ashame that they didn't love him enough to stop him from eating himself into an early grave because he killed himself with a knife, fork and being criminal." – Posted by Rufus Choate, AP/silive.com

On BuzzfeedNews.com via Facebook, so-called "Top Commenter" Joseph Raider, "Professor of Philosophy and Perceptions of Reailty at Kiss My Ass University, MSA," posted his alleged expert opinion about chokeholds:

"Greedy idiots, I hope they get nothing. The cops put the criminal in a rear-naked choke (very commonly used, even by children in j.j. classes) because he was resisting arrest, he died from past medical problems. I'd dismiss the case. The reason they use holds n shit and multiple cops is they can't just fight you or in this case the cop would just took out his baton and bashed his head in, he was trying to get him cuffed. I don't have sympathy for criminals or stupidity. All he woulda had to do is lay down n get cuffed, that's it"

Never mind that the use of chokeholds is barred by the New York Police Department's own rules.

Another "Top Commenter" named "Jen Yager Arnold" summed up his or her views about black men that are no doubt shared by a vast number of people:

"That man added no value to society, he had a long criminal re-
cird, was on parole and was blatantly outside a store selling loosies
illegally. He resisted arrested and due to his own actions is dead.
Get real ppl the guy was a no good loser that refused to follow the
law. The cops did not set out for him to die. They were trying to
arrest him. Those ops arenotbguilty and the NYPD is wrong to
pay the family."

Another unarmed black man, Freddie Gray, a 25-year old from Baltimore,
died of spinal cord injuries suffered in police custody after his arrest on
April 12, 2015, for the alleged possession of an illegal switchblade knife.

While riding in the police van, Gray became comatose. He was taken
to a trauma center, where he died a week later. His death on April 19, 2015,
initially resulted in peaceful protests and other related events. But on April
25, some of the protesting turned to violence. Unfortunately, on April 27,
2015, after his funeral, the city of Baltimore erupted into rioting and looting over several days by a small faction of troublemakers who either did
not comprehend or chose to ignore the enduring damage that their actions
will have on African-Americans as a whole.

As a result, a state of emergency was declared along with a six-day
curfew, while the National Guard was called to come in and take control
of the situation.

Again, commenters to news articles about the protests and unrest
found ways to blame the victim:

"The protesting, rioting and arson is over Freddie Gray, a repeat offending drug dealer. Funny how the vast vast majority of the people
receiving the "poor" treatment are long time criminals, attacking
police at the time, or both. If Freddie were white, we whites simply
wouldn't care, which is why most white neighborhoods are low crime
and why most black neighborhoods are high crime. Blacks repeatedly side with criminals against the police. We see it again and again.
They also maybe should have waited until the DA finished deciding

whether to file charges before burning stuff down, although getting a conviction on many of the charges filed is a complete pipe dream. No way is the driver of the van going to be convicted of murder 2. Not gonna happen. Total fantasy. Over 20 times Baltimore PD arrested old martyr Freddie the drug pusher and nothing bad happened to him. Seems to me they did pretty well with him overall.

Finally, if blacks in Baltimore suffer poor treatment, who's fault is that? Blacks in Baltimore are 63% of the population and as such are an undefeatable voting block. They can elect or defeat any city politician at will. They have both the government and the police force THEY CHOSE. This argument you are making might be worthy of consideration IF we were actually talking about a minority with no political power. We aren't, we are talking about a solid majority with complete and total control of Baltimore politics. If blacks in Baltimore failed in selecting the government that serves them then that's their fault. In any event they have complete control over the political process and can use said process to change the government anytime they like. There is no excuse whatsoever for rioting against the government they elected." – Posted by Mike Hughes, abcnews.go.com

A medical examiner ruled Gray's death a homicide, and on May 1, 2015, Baltimore City State's Attorney Marilyn Mosby announced that her office had filed charges against six police officers. A grand jury subsequently indicted the officers. The charges included various counts of manslaughter, misconduct in office for failure to perform a duty regarding the safety of a prisoner, and reckless endangerment.

One reader had this to say about the charges:

"It's a shame how 6 lives can be ruined by a common street thug. I hope the state's attorney looses her job over this." — Posted by Cut the B.S., wfsb.com (Eyewitness News 3, Hartford,Connecticut)

While it was good to see some measure of repercussion, many people will not be surprised if, as with scores of other deaths, it results in yet another acquittal.

It seems, though, that white men who are arrested have a different experience than black men. On Aug. 3, 2014, 18-year-old Steve Lohner walked the streets of Aurora, Colorado, with a loaded shotgun, claiming that he wanted to make the public "feel more comfortable around guns." He refused to show his ID and argued with the police. In the exchange between himself and law enforcement, he says in the video he posted on-line, that when asked about why he was carrying a loaded firearm, "For the defense of myself and those around me," citing his Second Amendment rights.

He was charged with obstruction, a misdemeanor, but police did not confiscate the loaded weapon and did not arrest Lohner.

The incident happened not far from where James Holmes killed 12 and wounded 70 people in a movie theater.

Bob Butler, the former NABJ president, noted a double standard. "You know that young man is alive today to talk about what happened to him. I would hate to think what would happen if a young black man was walking down the street with a shotgun and confronted by police to drop the gun, even though he wasn't pointing it at anybody," he said.

If recent tragedies are an indication, we know what would happen. In some instances, toy guns have caused the senseless deaths of young black men. On Nov. 22, 2014, Tamir Rice, of Cleveland was on a *playground* where he was *playing* with a toy gun that did not have the orange dot that identifies it as a replica. According to the article "Video of Police Shooting Boy Holding Toy Gun Is Released," published on abcnewsgo.com on Nov. 26, 2015, someone called 911 to report that a boy was waving a gun around, pulling it in and out of his pants and pointing at people. The caller said he wasn't sure if it was real or not.

Police went to investigate and claimed that Rice pulled the "gun" out of his waistband. The officers also said that he did not comply by "showing his hands" when they directed him to do so. Within scant seconds after the officers' car arrived on the scene, he was shot twice. In the message re-porting shooting Rice, the officer can be heard saying: "Shots fired. Male down. Black Male. Maybe 20." Tamir Rice was 12 years old.

In June 2015, Cleveland Municipal Court Judge Ronald Adrine found probable cause for the officers to be charged — Timothy Loehmann, who shot the boy to be charged with murder, involuntary manslaughter, reck-less homicide, and other offenses, and his partner, Frank Garmback, with negligent homicide and dereliction of duty.

A comment from the USA Today article "Officer in Tamir Rice shoot-ing: 'He gave me no choice,'" published on June 14, 2015, via Facebook gave a startling view as someone who did not think people should be sym-pathetic to Rice's death and did not appear to care that his real name is on it.

"Of course the media finds the MOST cherub faced picture of the criminal to print! Lies are of comision AND omission. These are lies of comission!

Do a google search and see him posing like a gansta flashing "signs"! Look at the photo showing him walking with a gun in his hand, albeit an airsoft gun, a police office could EASILY at a distance not be able to tell the difference.

And SEE that the judge that made the ruling is BLACK, which as we know, couldn't have ANY bias, wink, wink! Just as the Obama Justice Departtment under Holder has gone after EVERY JURY descision AGAINST a black man, that has become HIGHLY PUBLIC!" – Posted by Jim Flowers, via Facebook.com

Rice did not have a criminal record. I also searched Google and found three photos of the 12-year-old posing with two fingers on both hands in a sideways "V" sign. In one where he is with two other people, he was wearing a blue polo shirt. Another was of him alone doing the same pose, and the last one shows him in a white T-shirt and a baseball cap displaying a one-handed sideways "V" sign. While I know very little of gang culture, the signs do not look like the complicated digit-bending configurations that I have seen. I think Flowers makes this assumption in order to bolster his negative opinions. Another reality is that a lot of kids use hand gestures in photos to look "cool" and may even wear colors associated with gangs, but it does not always mean that they are in gangs.

On July 10, 2015, an Ohio appeals court panel said that it would not force Judge Adrine to issue arrest warrants for the officers. The case was still pending.

Twenty-two-year old John Crawford was similarly holding a toy rifle when he was killed in a Beavercreek, Ohio, Walmart. According to "Cops shoot and kill man holding toy gun in Wal-Mart," published Aug. 9, 2014, on MSNBC.com, Crawford was killed on Aug. 4, 2014.

LeeCee Johnson, his girlfriend and mother of his children, with whom he was on a cell phone call when he was shot, said he had been playing video games. While still on the phone, he went to the toy gun section, where he apparently picked up a BB gun to purchase and carried it around as he continued shopping in other departments.

A customer in the store called police to report that a man was walking around with a gun. Police arrived and spotted him at some point. Police reports state that Crawford did not put down the weapon as instructed, and officers opened fire, killing him.

The article "Man police shot in Walmart killed over fake gun, family says," published on daytondailynews.com on Aug. 6, 2014, discussed Crawford's death and the family's plan to get the NAACP involved. The article included an interview with his children's mother. This comment to the article presented a glaringly negative view of the victim, making up facts and inventing scenarios to justify the shooting:

"Lets see here. They go to Walmart and for whatever idiotic reason he grabs, I suppose a toy gun from the shelf, and I am guessing takes it out of the packaging. I think most come in some kind of card board packaging, then starts waiving it around pointing at people to the point were folks in the store sure must have thought it was a real gun since they called 911 to report that very thing. Im sure a commotion was started and people were getting the heck out of there. And at no time during this did this guy think... Hey Im waiving a toy gun around ???why???? freaking people out. Maybe I shouldnt do that??? Or maybe the cops are gonna get called... And then of course when they do he still is waiving it around refusing to put it down.???? Why?????what was the goal here. What normal person would do this?? why would anyone do this to the point of causing a panic in the first place and then when the police come you still are doing it and wont put it down as ordered.. .. That said dont be surprised that you get shot for your efforts. This guy made the decisions to act like he did and those actions and decisions led to his death. HIS ACTIONS AND HIS DECISIONS. So his babys mamma and or the girlfriend and baby momma to be can call the NAACP Jessie Jackson and try to make it racial all you want. Call Santa Clause if you want but the bottom line is this. He made the choice to act like he did and his actions caused the outcome. Lets not forget that his actions is what started this entire sequence of events and contributed to the death of a truly innocent woman who suffered a heart attack due Im sure in part to the stress of the incident when she was in the store. An incident that HE and HE alone chose to start. That is it period. The officers actions were just and correct. Good job. Im sorry that you have to go through this but you did the right thing. never forget that." – Posted by jjjjjjj, Daytondailynews.com

None of the stories about the shooting say that Crawford was waving the gun around at people, and so the poster is wrong there. The initial caller to 911, Ronald Ritchie, did originally report that Crawford was pointing the gun at people walking by, but later recanted in an interview with the Guardian, saying, "At no point did he shoulder the rifle and point it at somebody." The "gun" in question was in fact an unpackaged BB/pellet air rifle.

The commenter clearly had more sympathy for a woman who reportedly had a fatal heart attack during the Walmart melee. However, the message that black people cause our own problems is prevalent in these reader comments.

Neither of the two officers was indicted by a grand jury in the shooting. Although they were initially put on administrative duties, they are back at work. The Crawford family filed a wrongful death lawsuit against Walmart and the police seeking damages in excess of $75,000. As of August 2015, the lawsuit was still pending.

In the summer of 1977, after the historic blackout that nearly crippled New York City on July 13-14, I remember running around the backyard in Roosevelt, Long Island, with my foster brothers yelling, "Son of Sam!" pretending to have guns and to shoot at each other. We didn't know any better. But my mother did. She was extremely angry when she came out into that backyard and yelled at us to stop.

We were doing that because all we kept hearing on the television news was about the manhunt for the serial killer dubbed "The Son of Sam" who had between 1976 and July 1977 randomly killed six people and wounded seven. My mother told us that "Son of Sam" was a bad person for killing people and that it was very bad for us to imitate what he did.

Although I cannot recall so many years later *exactly* what else she said, much of it had to do the negative things that guns represented, and it scared us and made us embarrassed over what we had been pretending to do.

It was punishment enough because that parental reproach was so thorough, it at least made me never want to *look* at guns, *play* with guns or *pretend* to have a gun ever again. That lesson carried over into my adulthood, and I never allowed my son to play with a toy gun, nor have I ever given one as a gift to any male child. Perhaps my mother knew then, what we all have come to know now — that things do not end well for a black person with a gun, no matter how innocent they might be.

In reality, many of the young men who died holding toy guns were racially profiled to some degree. I do wonder whether there is more urgency on the receiving end of a 911 call when a black man is alleged to have a gun. Now, it appears that regardless of age, black hands are considered far more threatening around a breakable molded plastic trigger than white hands are.

Racial profiling, especially in "stop and frisk" jurisdictions like New York City, where police disproportionately single out people of color for such special attention, is a decades-old, hot-button topic. On Aug. 12, 2013, U.S. District Judge Shira Scheindlin ruled the NYPD's stop-and-frisk policy was unconstitutional. In the same month, the New York City Council passed two profiling bills known as the Community Safety Act that required the creation of an inspector general's office to oversee the NYPD and allow victims of the outrageous practice to sue the city.

It is widely known that African-Americans are disproportionately stopped by the police. In 2012, the NYPD reported that of the 532,911 people stopped in New York, 284,229 were black, 165,140 were Latino, and 50,366 were white.

The New York Daily News article "NYPD targets minorities in stop and frisk: report" published May 9, 2012, focused on a New York Civil Liberties Union (NYCLU) critical analysis about the NYPD's controversial program. According to its findings, although blacks and Hispanics comprised just 14 percent of the population in six NYPD precincts, they still accounted for more than 70 percent of the stops.

According to the NYCLU analysis, nearly nine out of 10 New Yorkers who were stopped and frisked were completely innocent.

Jumaane Williams, city councilman for Brooklyn's 45th district, helped to push through the two Community Safety bills, and has continually been a critic of NYPD's overuse of stop-and-frisk, saying that there was "no concrete connection between increased use of the measure and the cessation of crime."

Some commenters, presumably black, taunted the NYPD for being so scared of "dark-skinned" young men. Other rants, like these two, insulted minorities and praised stop and frisk:

"The ACLU & the dolts posting here just can't admit that the policies of the NYPD, including S&F, have reduced the crime rate in NYC to historically low levels. The police ARE stopping the right people! Patdowns DO reduce the number of guns being carried on the street! Proactive policing works!"-Posted by BIGJAKE, NYDailynews.com

"It is more demeaning to be gunned down by a thug in your own community than it is to have a chat with a police officer that's less invasive than getting screened by the TSA. The only people who ask why they are being stopped are usually the ones with something to hide, hence their nervousness about the reason for the stop. If you don't have anything to hide, the cops frisk you and you're gone in 2 minutes, and the streets are safer as a result." – Posted by murraysilverman, NYDailynews.com

Later in the comment thread, the same person let loose with this bomb, which sounded suspiciously like slave masters who wanted to believe their servants were actually happy and better off for being enslaved:

"All of the blacks and hispanics that work for me tell me how grateful they are that the NYPD has a heavy presence in their neighborhoods. They think stop and frisk may be inconvenient, but they appreciate it since it helps police get the bad guys off the street. Most blacks and hispanics actually support stop and frisk, but the rabble rousers in their community along with liberal anti-police groups have the loudest voices." – Posted by murraysilverman, NYDailynews

By 2013, of the 191,558 people stopped in New York, 104,958 were black, 55,191 were Latino, and 20,877 were white. Less than a year after the City Council passed the bills, the NYPD reported that at the beginning of 2014, 46,235 people were stopped, 24,777 of them black, 12,622 Latino, and 5,536 of them white.

Then Mayor Michael Bloomberg was visibly upset and vowed to veto the bills, but the Council voted to override his attempts to do so.

Even though it was his prerogative to veto them, it was his shocking response to the bills that inadvertently "outed" him as a racist. It has always been his opinion that stop-and-frisk lowered crime in New York. During a broadcast on his weekly radio show, he told his audience: "One newspaper and one news service, they just keep saying, 'Oh, it's a disproportionate percentage of a particular ethnic group.' That may be. But it's not a disproportionate percentage of those who witnesses and victims describe as committing the murders."

He continued, "In that case, incidentally, I think, we disproportionately stop whites too much and minorities too little," Bloomberg said. "It's exactly the reverse of what they're saying. I don't know where they went to school, but they certainly didn't take a math course, or a logic course."

His comments were upsetting because it sounded as though he was saying innocent blacks and Latinos deserved to be stopped. He was speaking for himself and those of his ilk. The Rev. Al Sharpton followed up by saying that Bloomberg should apologize or clarify his statement, a request that the mayor did not honor, and some online responses to news articles about his statements backed him up:

"The Mayor has nothing to apologize for! Based on the statistics, there is nothing unreasonable about the percentage of stop-and-frisk of blacks or Latinos. Black and Latinos *are suspected of causing of 90% of murders in NYC.* Stop-and frisk, based on statistics, is properly implemented, Smart job NYPD! The numbers showed that 87% of the people stopped under stop-and-frisk in 2012 were black or Latino, and that 9% were white. That same year, more than 90% of those identified as murder suspects were blacks or Latino; just 7% were white." – Posted by StatenIslander, NYDailynews.com

A few days after the federal ruling on stop-and-frisk, Sybrina Fulton, Trayvon Martin's mother, spoke out against the practice. Even though her son's murder did not take place in New York, the 17-year-old was a victim of racial profiling — not by police, but by the neighborhood watch volunteer who confronted him.

In a statement on NBC's "Meet the Press," she said, "You can't give people the authority, whether it's a civilian or police officers, the right to stop somebody just because of the color of their skin."

Comments to an article about that TV appearance published in the New York Daily News were very unkind to her. They said things like, "If she focused more on raising her son that he might still be here" and that she was "using his death" to garner sympathy.

Someone using the screen name "ArodsAlbatrossContract" wrote an extremely long rant about how most white people are "not born" to be racist, but that black people are "absolutely" raised to be racist. It said in part:

"If Trayvon Martin was a good kid - I'd be first on line to say he was. But he wasnt. I know the black community would love to believe that he was a good kid, but anyone whos black with a modicum of informed intelligence(which is a small percentage mind you) knows he was a punk in the making. He had a twitter acount entitled "No_Limit_Ni**a" which was fraught with references to FIGHTING, DRUGS, MISOGYNY, RACISM and DRUG DEALING. He also talked about his Mom kicking him out of the house. He also had a Myspace account which showed pics of him holding handguns. Dont believe me? Do a simple Google search. He was suspended for 10 days from school for having a bag full of stolen jewelry. He was a typical Black punk who lacked parenting. THATS WHY he's dead. Because he Messed with the wrong guy. Someone who WAS NOT white by ANY persons standards besides the hyper liberal media which is SOLELY responsible for this being turned into a "white" on Black crime.

Then you have the Race baiting slimeballs in Jackson and Sharpton who further prove their ignorance by turnign this garbage into a hate whitey event.

STOP AND FRISK? I wonder why. Because as long as I can re-member Blacks and Hispanics in NY are the cause of most violent crimes, most thefts, most drug dealings --- should I go on?"

(I would venture to say that this person came from an actual hate site and wanted to stir up the masses and unfortunately, many people agreed with that person.)

"Great... comments from The Worlds Worst Mother on police procedure. Why did you abandon your kid? Get in the way of your crackhead life?

Black and Hispanic males make up over 90% of the violent crime perps in NYC. That's rape, robbery, assault and murder, and that's a fact." – Posted by Zulka Sunderland, NYDailynews.com

The worst part about stop-and-frisk is that African-American boys and men have to be subjected to a different type of parental discussion in addi-tion to the "birds and bees" talk about sex. They are often told, or should be told, that their image can get them killed, no matter how positive they perceive themselves to be. It matters not whether they are wearing a hood-ed sweatshirt or suit and tie. It doesn't matter whether they walk with the "baggy jean" shuffle or confident swagger, how they wear their hair, or whether they have long dreadlocks or are bald.

In her ruling, Judge Scheindlin said that New York police officers were "too quick to deem innocent behaviors" as suspicious, which in turn "watered down" the "legal standard" required for someone to be stopped. She further noted that officers stopped blacks on "lesser degrees of objectivity founded on suspicion than whites" for things like furtive movements and having pocket bulges that in all probability were the result of carrying cell phones and wallets, not firearms.

For those young and adult black men who do not have a criminal background, being stopped (and possibly killed) just on the premise of suspicion is degrading. The vast majority of those stopped were guilty of doing nothing more than walking down a street and maybe changing their minds about which direction they wanted to go to get to their destination. The bottom line is that racial profiling of any kind is wrong, no matter how much anyone who is for the practice tries to justify it.

Perhaps nothing brings out closet racists more than stories about statistics that indicate African-Americans, men in particular, have been and continue to be targets of discrimination. The Wall Street Journal published "Racial Gap in Men's Sentencing" on Feb. 14, 2013, about the U.S. Sentencing Commission analysis that found that prison sentences of black men were nearly 20 percent longer than those of white men for similar crimes. One respondent, identified as Peter Maggio, drew his own conclusions:

> "The truth is that blacks are more criminal-minded. We white men in fact chain blacks up for their own benefit. In jail, they learn to rehabilitate and appreciate Western culture. There is no need to sentence white men to long prison terms. White men can learn from their mistakes faster and the white community will rein him in through social pressure. The black men have longer rap sheets."

He no doubt found his remarks amusing.

News stories that include statistical data divided by race are certain to draw bigoted remarks to comment forums faster than if it were was about an academically gifted black male child who comes from a two-parent home in the suburbs.

Although "Job Losses Show Wider Racial Gap in New York," a July 12, 2009, article in The New York Times was not about crime, it documents that unemployment for African-Americans during the recession had increased faster than it did for whites.

Using statistics from the city comptroller's office in New York City, the article stated that at the end of the first quarter in March 2008: "There were more than 80,000 more unemployed blacks than whites, according to the report, even though there are roughly 1.5 million more whites than blacks here."

The story also said that economists were not certain why so many more blacks were losing their jobs in New York, and that a large share of the layoffs that were taking place were in fields where blacks were not well represented, such as finance and professional services.

Frank Braconi, the chief economist in the city comptroller's office, was quoted in the story as saying: "African-Americans have been hit disproportionally hard. The usual pattern is that the unemployment rate among African-Americans tends to be twice as high as for non-Hispanic whites, but the gap has widened substantially in the city during the past year."

This story was a breeding ground for racist responses.

One commenter for this story smugly repackaged his or her racism in "intellectual" tones with pride, disregarding racism as a factor in the disparities that African-Americans face on a daily basis:

"No surprise that unemployment would be higher for blacks simply because they don't generally have the education level as whites do. Many will try to say it's a racial issue, but it's just plain economics and logic. I'm certain many in the media will claim its racial, but it would only be racial if you laid off whites to keep blacks simply because they were black. Most companies will lay off those of lowest seniority, lowest education and keep those with the best work reliability regardless of what color they are." – Posted by Vince Hugh, Atlanta, NYTimes.com

A commenter identified as Bill Garrett said that the "probable reason" for the racial disparities in the unemployment gap was that businesses were shamed into hiring blacks that they did not really want to hire.

He wrote in part:

"The reality is that all the laws, affirmative action and 'political correctness' under the sun will not change how people really feel in their hearts."

Garrett may unfortunately be correct in his assumptions that people may never change their views about African-Americans, but sometimes change in behavior is forced into existence.

It is no surprise that crime stories involving African-Americans bring out the worst in those who comment on news stories online.

An article in the New York Daily News, "Columbia torture victim identifies defendant in court," on June 9, 2008, about a black man who raped and tortured a white Columbia University student in New York allowed racist readers to get into their comfort zone. Online comments to the story offered words like "evil," "savage," "monster," and "animal." Many suggested "castration" — an ever-present threat — as the solution to stopping black men and their future male children from ever doing anything wrong.

"What you people don't realize is that we are surrounded by animals like this and there are always going to be more and more of them...and many are little children right now...being raised to hate whites with such a passion that they don't see whites as human beings. All of your hatred toward those who are caught isn't going to stop this tide of sickness and hate. I don't know what is. Violence in movies, TV and video games doesn't help. Schools should teach compassion instead of the poor job they do in teaching reading and writing." – Posted by Anonymous Poster, NYDailynews.com

Readers of the article "Man Scared Woman to Death, Police Say," from the Associated Press, on Jan. 29, 2009, responded to the mug shot photo of a dark-complexioned man with dreadlocks with racist remarks about his physical appearance and referred to old stereotypes in the South.

"I feel this a reverse hate (?) crime! He took advantage of his black-ness to impose his will on a helpless white elderly woman. He should have known she hadn't seen a black man in her house since she was 10 and his name was Jeeves (the family bathroom atten-dant). At the sight of this coward, she was paralyzed. I would prob-ably die of a heart attack as well if I found a 200-pound baboon with a gun in my living room! Here's hoping you do...so you will. You're too stupid to live." – Posted by Dbgarcia17D, news.aol.com

It is likely that the comedian Sandra Bernhard killed her career when as part of her show in September 2008 she suggested that then Republican vice-presidential nominee Sarah Palin would be "gang-raped by my big black brothers" if she came to Manhattan. In her mea culpa, Bernhard, who is Jewish, denied it. She said, "The [gang rape comment] is part of a much larger, nuanced, and yes, provocative (that's what I do) piece from my show about racism, freedom, women's rights, and the extreme views of Alaskan Gov. Sarah Palin, a woman who doesn't believe that other women should have the right to choose."

That did not help Bernhard recover from using a stereotype from which black men recoil on a daily basis — especially after her monologue started appearing on YouTube. While some readers of the Nov. 11, 2008, New York Daily News story "Sandra Bernhard denies issuing Sarah Palin 'gang rape' warning" about the video strayed off-topic, others somewhat condoned her comments:

"I think the video should be released that contains the phrase concerning the "black brothas". I suspect she actually did say "gang RAPE." Sadly, as I'm aware of crime statistics, that it's not a terribly unlikelt scenario." – Posted by Nietzschean, NYDailynews.com

Relatively often, the online commenters attribute the so-called inbred proclivity for misbehavior by black men to their African ancestry and present a narrow, bigoted view of Africa, citing lack of "civilization" there.

When South African President Thabo Mbeki was forced out of office in 2008, in responses to "South African ruling party mulls fate of President Thabo Mbeki," Sept. 21, 2008, in the Chicago Tribune, many readers cast him as a corrupt politician with no ability or aptitude as a ruler, while other readers gave their best example of historical "facts."

"At least in South Africa they dont cut heads off and put them on stick posts or eat enemies. No but South African coons *do* cut the hands off and eyes out of small children to make medicine and also rape 3 month old infants to cure themselves of HIV infection, amongst other diabolical acts." – Posted by Nick, Glen Ellyn, IL, ChicagoTribune.com

Former Detroit Mayor Kwame Kilpatrick, who was impeached and removed from the office in 2008 and jailed for 100 days as a result of a highly public sex scandal and his handling of whistleblower bailouts, was released early. Although he had a plea deal and served his time, many readers of the Associated Press story "Former Detroit Mayor Released From Jail," Feb. 3, 2009, gave the beleaguered politician no mercy.

Some readers somehow drew African ancestry into the discussion in predicting that black people would automatically reelect him, despite his conviction.

"Don't worry, he'll run for mayor of Detroit and win again. I'm from Louisiana and the African monkeys ALWAYS put the worst candidate back into office in New Orleans. Why should they be any different in Detroit?" – Posted byPjbohn985, NYDailynews.com

Another said:

"and the Idiots would re-elect him if giving the chance.-this is the new face of every metro area mayor.--the socialist/democrat/communist agenda is working briliantly!--pay them to have more babies and have working americans pay for them and penalize working Americans for having children!--they are out breeding us so they can out vote us!----keep on working america!--millions on welfare are depending on you!" – Posted by NYC5577, NYDailynews.com

And another:

"If this was A white Person F--king a, N----R Instead of a N----R, F--k ing a white Woman He would Have been Sent to Federal Prison and spent about 10 years before being on Probation. N----r Politicians have a Diffrent Get out of Jail card, Because no one wants another La Watts, Chicago and Other N** *R, Riots To happen. If the White People in America Keep F*****g N*****S, Then there will be No White People Here. White People are a Majority in America, N*****s, Are Now a very small Majority In America, Hispanics and Orientals, and Other Illegal, Aliens Are now the Majority. And they Don't F***K N-----S. Or White People. Breeding will Eventually Make us Extinct. I am 65 years old. If my Two Daughters came home, Pregnant by a *N*****R, Her, the baby and The, N****R. Would have Been in the Kunta Kinte Boiling Pot. White people need to Make More White Babiess, and their, Babies Need to get The Message that When they Look at their Children, They're not looking at a Ni*rR." – Posted by Pjbohn985, news.aol.com

Even when black men are singled out in the media for accomplishments, the cyber commentary often takes an ugly turn. When Fanhouse.com, a sports news website, profiled the Pittsburgh Steelers' Santonio Holmes, it failed if it was trying to pay him a compliment. The article on Feb. 2, 2009, was headlined "Holmes' Late Heroics Win Steelers Title: He used to sell drugs on a corner."

Holmes' skills won his team the 2009 Super Bowl and earned him the coveted MVP title. Readers responding to the online article essentially "ran away" with the "used to sell drugs" subtitle like a freight train without brakes. The article was heavy on football lingo and highlights of the game, but the subhead opened up an online can of worms like this one, diminishing the bright light that Holmes' personal milestone represented:

> "Great game, but is there any black athlete who is not a former drug dealer, gang member, gun carrying bar hoping thug, playing in the NFL? If there is then let those three guys step forward.. Is there any NFL black player who got into college by having a high stat score? If there is then let that one guy step forward, Just how did these thugs get into college when they can't even speak? yet alone pass an eighth grade equivalent test is beyond reason. Something is wrong here. I thing the Super Bowl should change its name to the Ghetto Bowl. It won't be long till half the players are suspended for carrying guns, bar fights, shootings, and just simple armed robbery even though they make millions. Other than that, a great game." – Posted by Richymack, fanhouse.aol.com

Holmes has acknowledged that he sold drugs as a teenager in his hometown of Belle Glade, Florida. It's an old story that he refers back to from time to time. He said his mother's support and guidance helped him achieve his triumph as a professional football player.

It seems to be much easier for readers to accept the stereotype that all African-Americans athletes are criminally minded, despite their success. There are plenty of examples that debunk this myth. Cleveland Cavaliers basketball player LeBron James, who announced plans in 2015 to partner with the University of Akron to guarantee four-year scholarships to as many as 1,100 local students, is one of them, and so is Tennessee Titans football player Michael Oher, whose success story was the inspiration for the 2009 biographical film "The Blind Side."

CHAPTER 7

Mama's Little Babies

"Wait, the most shocking part of that story is that one of these kids actually knows who her father is." – Posted by Guest, NYDailynews.com, Dec. 7, 2007

BIGOTS WHO COMMENT ON NEWS stories seem to love nothing more than to vent their utter surprise that black children have fathers who are visibly a part of their lives, whether married to the child's mother or not. When a black father saw a video of his daughter attacking a white passenger on a New York subway train with a group of other girls in 2007, he did what a parent of any race should have done: He turned her into the police.

It is understandably mortifying for any parent to see public proof their own child has been involved in a racially motivated or criminal act of any kind. Although the father might not have been able to provide a protective legal shell, as many affluent whites can, he demonstrated his parental responsibility.

Those who commented on the New York Daily News article "Dad Sorry for 'A' Train Teen's Actions" on Dec. 7, 2007, were not entirely sympathetic to his attempt to set his child on the right path. In questioning why any educated man's child would act in such a manner, this reader sets up the angry black woman stereotype. Angry white children generally are called "rebels," while angry black children are called the "N-word" and compared to animals.

"Feel bad for the parents, but the thug women here are animals....
hey Al Sharton and Jesse where are you now? here are your nappy
headed ho's," –Posted by ralph316, NYDailynews.com

While some readers praised the father's actions, some imply that only
black teenagers act out in public. It may just be that white teenagers are
not caught as much or the public turns a blind eye to them.

"Why do I always see black teenagers creating trouble in public
more than kids of any other race. I think the law on teen agers is
way too lenient and promotes 'I will do what I want, and u cant do
nothing, infact after I assault you, I will call the cops and they take
you' attitude." – Posted by kashmira, NYDailynews.com

"Why are we concerned about a dad? i thought black kids have
single moms??" – Posted by ab97777, NYDailynews.com

It would probably make life simpler if women were required to check a box
on birth certificate applications for black babies that say "ghetto child" or
"non-ghetto child." This way the countless academic journals and studies that make sweeping assertions about black children could distinguish
between those who have poor, uneducated black mothers and criminally
minded fathers and those who do not.

I was raised — from about age 5 to 12 — in the Long Island suburb
Roosevelt by two working parents. It was in a middle-class neighborhood
with mostly working-class black families, along with a family of white hip-
pies and the Hardekopfs, an elderly German couple next door to us.

I never paid attention to the differences between the behaviors of
black children in the "inner city" and those of my more-fortunate school-
mates. Honestly, I think that I did not know any so-called "ghetto" children, and I had no concept of what that was until I was much older. I later
learned that the term was not limited to Brooklyn, the Bronx, Queens, and
Harlem. "Ghetto" was, in fact, anywhere economically challenged blacks

lived in segregated enclaves — whether that was in Baltimore, Georgia, Los Angeles, or another city or state.

In online comments, it seems that black children, especially those in urban areas, are considered a particularly doomed subset.

Michael Days, the Philadelphia Daily News editor, recalled the comments after a story about a fatal accident involving three black children published July 25, 2014, on Philly.com.

According to the article, three children, their mother, and another adult were selling fruit on a busy corner in a North Philadelphia neighborhood to raise money to build a playground next to a church.

"The children were all killed when two knuckleheads carjacked a realtor," Days told me. "They took the car and the tire blows and the car runs into these kids on a corner selling this fruit, and into the mother and this other person. How sympathetic a story is that? The whole city had lost their minds over this thing."

When the story about the funeral, "Hundreds mourn 3 children killed by carjacked SUV," was posted to their website, on Aug. 4, 2014, he said the responses blew everyone's mind. Someone commented: "Well thank you for curbing the breed."

Daily News staff members expressed disgust over the racist commentary.

"At the time, it was so horrible, to the point where white people were like coming to my office saying what are we going to do?" Days said. "…When it gets to the point where people are coming to your door, saying 'I cannot take this,' you know that it's really over the top."

This is a perfect example about how deeply online racist comments affect people of any race. It becomes a domino effect of emotions whereby anyone who is affected by racist words wants to believe that the writers cannot be serious about what they are saying.

Days said that the comment was eventually removed from the website, but it took some doing.

"You have to call someone at Philly.com, and they have to react to it," he said. "It's hard to justify it. A lot of people are — beyond black, white and whatever — they're just embarrassed. Decent people are embarrassed."

Even when the story is not a tragedy such as this one, comments to news articles about parents who are raising children in urban ghettos continue to build a negative bridge of hatred against African-Americans. Without knowing all of the circumstances, it is easier for bigots to "cherry pick" everything that a black child supposedly does wrong — whether it is the improper use of a word or the recitation of violent rap lyrics verbatim. Either way, racists don't like black children.

For decades, issues about the parenting habits of African-Americans, mostly those who are not middle-class, have been a politically charged public arena. President Obama, Bill Cosby, and many other prestigious blacks have tackled the controversial subject.

Cora Daniels, in her book "Ghettonation: Dispatches from America's Culture War" (Broadway Books, 2008), pointed out that some of the very same behaviors for which "ghetto" blacks are loathed were embraced and celebrated by middle-class suburban whites.

Nonconformists like Microsoft founder Bill Gates and Apple co-founder Steve Jobs could drop out of college, put on their coats and ties, and rule the world. It doesn't quite work the same way for blacks.

In New York, bodegas or "corner stores" owned by nonblack immigrants are commonplace in black neighborhoods. Both the blacks and the immigrants are victims of racism, but young black people are more likely to be perceived as threats. In one case in Brooklyn, a Yemeni storeowner beat a teenager in the back of the head with a hammer because the man thought the boy and his friends had stolen from him and had attacked a sleeping store employee. The case was reported in "East New York bodega owner indicted in hammer attack," April 13, 2008, New York Daily News. In comments about the incident, some readers endorsed cracking the skull of a 14-year-old male black child with a hammer as a fitting punishment.

"The store owner had a right to defend himself from these punks. Why should he sit back while they beat the **** out of his employee. Apparently the only time someone is allowed to defend themselves is after an innocent man has been maimed or killed. There are consequences to one's action and this kid got what was coming to him, if this happened more often, there might be a few more boyz actually leaving da' hood for something better. Instead, everyone pulls the race card as an excuse for acting like a bunch of fools. I don't care how old this *** was, if he's old enough to rob and steal, then he's old enough to take a hammer to the head." – Posted by jpd57, NYDailynews.com

The Daily News story also described the victim as an aspiring basketball player. Many of those commenting used as an opportunity to diminish the accomplishments of black professional basketball players in general and to ridicule those who aspire to basketball careers, a dream that is not limited to blacks from poor neighborhoods.

"What BS about his basketball playing skills making him some sort of ghetto saint. Our colleges and the NBA are full of black basketball playing punks. Hitting these savages over the head with a hammer seems to be the only way to get the message across to them." – Posted by Heddick, NYDailynews.com

The May 27, 2008, Daily News article "East Flatbush mom learned how to read so she could answer her son" was about a Caribbean woman who came to America for a better life. She conquered her illiteracy so that she would be able to read to her two children and be a better parent. Instead of praise, admiration, or empathy, her story drew cruel responses from readers.

"Another fine argument for sealing the borders. Instead of literacy partners, she should have been sent to Planned Parenthood straight off the banana boat. What a heart-warming story, another illiterate having ******* children that my tax dollars will have to incarcerate." – Posted by uberchristian, NYDailynews.com

The unfortunate murder in Brooklyn of a 16-year-old girl by her 15-year-old cousin who was alleged to be mentally unstable elicited some initial sympathy from readers. Responses to the Daily News stories in early October 2008 — "Teen girl fatally knifed in Brooklyn" and "Teen in Shannon Braithwaite Brooklyn stabbing horror called troubled" — blamed her parents, crack, and the ramifications of "ghetto" behavior.

> "lock this ghetto trash up. Trash breeds trash." – Posted by Sus, NYDailynews.com

When a white, mentally unstable child or teen is in the news, the debate seems to center on the help that the child needs. It seems, though, that when it is a black child or teen in the same situation, it seems that mostly racist sentiments pour out online.

> "I said it once and I will say it again...this is TNB (typical n1gg@r behavior). Only these animal porch monkeys can think of acting out such a henious crime. We should send these punks to Afghanistan and drop them in the middle of a Taliban controlled village to see just how tough they really are. Perhaps their throats will be the ones being slashed by the Taliban psychotics." – Posted by Why Me Worry?, NYDailynews.com

The article "Time to profile white men?" on Salon.com about mass shootings by mostly young white men was a controversial query by journalist Jeff Sirota. The subjects of the story included 20-year-old Adam Lanza, who killed 20 children and six adults at Sandy Hook Elementary School in Newtown, Connecticut, and who also shot and killed his mother and himself in December 2012.

It is unlikely that young white men would be profiled as young black men have been over the years. The double standard over criminality continues.

Noted clinical psychologist Jeff Gardere, interviewed by Newsone. com reporter Lynette Holloway for her story "Mental Health Expert: Parents Must Stop Being in Denial About Kids, Violence," was asked about Sirota's Salon story. He said in part: "I don't make it a point of stereotyping anyone because two wrongs don't make a right. We know at the Virginia Tech shooting that was an Asian young man. In another shooting, it was based on someone's religious grounds, so it's not productive to look at this as a white male problem," he said.

Six young black men were arrested for the Dec. 4, 2006, assault of a white student at a high school in Jena, Louisiana. Reportedly, before the assault, the school had been the scene of racially charged incidents, ranging from nooses found hanging from trees in the school courtyard to the outbreak of fires in the building. The black students were charged with aggravated battery, conspiracy to commit aggravated battery, and simple battery in the assault case.

African-Americans protested the treatment of the young black men, dubbed the "Jena Six," as discriminatory, compared to the treatment of the young white men involved. On Jan. 20, 2007, nearly 20 protesters participated in a civil rights march on Jena, considered the largest demonstration in central Louisiana in years.

A year later, one member of the Jena Six attempted suicide after being arrested and accused of shoplifting. In the Associated Press story "'Jena Six' Teen Shoots Self, Survives" of Dec. 30, 2008, an officer interviewed for the story said that the young man did it because he didn't want to be "in the news again." The young man also had been accused of resisting arrest and simple assault. The 18-year-old student, Mychal Bell, who later pleaded guilty to a juvenile charge of attempted second-degree murder, was the only one tried for assault in the original case. In the Jan. 15, 2009, CNN article "Jena 6's Mychal Bell: Pressure led to suicide try," the student admitted to a suicide attempt. He had, according to the online story, "strived to do well after Jena" and said that the Dec. 24, 2009, shoplifting allegations had "devastated" him.

Some readers who commented on the Associated Press story argued that he had failed since the incident to take advantage of his "second chance at life."

"In all the screaming, wailing, and gnashing of teeth about the "unfair treatment" of the Jena 6, all too many people have forgotten that they're really nothing but violent, anti-social thugs." – Posted by Jchowell3657, NYDailynews.com

For the duration of the Jena 6 incident, no racist stereotype went unmentioned in posts. Even Bell's first name, "Mychal," did not escape criticism. When Stormfront.org re-posted "Mychal Bell of 'Jena Six' Ordered Back To Jail" in July 2007, to the website, one forum member had to add this:

"Really, though, how in the world does one name a male child something embarrassing like "Mychal" and expect him NOT to lead a life of shiftlessness and degeneracy?

Can you see it on a resume, even? Though maybe a rose by any other name…" – Posted by Green-Eyed Lady, stormfront.org

The name "Mychal" Bell is now immortalized on his bachelor's degree from Southern University in Baton Rouge, Louisiana.

In 2009, five of the Jena 6 pleaded no contest to the charge of attempted murder of the white student beaten in the racially charged incident. They also paid restitution to the victim and his family, who had sued each of the black men involved in the case. Bell was convicted as an "adult criminal" for his role in the beating of a white classmate, freed, and then ordered to spend 18 months at a juvenile facility because of a parole violation for prior convictions.

Although readers branded them as career criminals, they have had the ultimate revenge by changing the course of their lives. Nearly all finished high school and attended college. Robert Bailey and Bryant Purvis both graduated from Grambling State University. Jesse Ray Beard attended Hofstra University; Theo Shaw graduated from the University of Louisiana at Monroe.

The lives of those young men from Jena turned out better than the lives of the "Central Park 5." The four black men and one Hispanic man were wrongfully convicted of the rape and assault of a white woman in New York's Central Park in 1989. All of them spent several years in jail, the eldest nearly 14. Although their sentences were vacated in 2002 after another man confessed to the crime, they never quite recovered from the racial stigma.

In 2003, the five sued the city of New York for malicious prosecution, racial discrimination, and emotional distress. In 2014, they reached a $41 million settlement, made a reality by Mayor Bill de Blasio. When the mayor revealed how he and his African-American wife, Chirlane McCray, have spoken to their son, Dante, about racial profiling after the death of Eric Garner, some readers were not sympathetic to the couple's concerns for their biracial child. The story "N.Y. Mayor Bill de Blasio spoke bluntly on race, policing in ways harder for Obama," on Dec. 5, 2014, compared how the New York City mayor and President Obama spoke about racism to the public. Commenters seemed to thumb their noses at the idea that Dante had anything to fear with comments like these:

"I am ashamed that NYC is represented by such a buffoon as DeBlasio. The only danger his Son Dante faces these days is failing all his courses at Brooklyn Tech (which I graduated from when walking through Fort Greene Park meant having a death wish). And unless Dante is majoring in how to become a thug like Michael Brown his only contact with police will be the ones who drive him around the city.

It's time that Obama, DeBlasio and their liberal ilk put away the race card. Most people in America do not have relatives that can be traced back to slavery unless you perhaps go back to Roman times. In America it's been over 150 years since the slaves were freed at the cost of hundreds of thousands of Union soldier lives. So please give it a break." – Posted by TiredOfBeingTaxedToDeath, WashingtonPost.com

"Because Chirlane and I have had to talk to Dante for years about the dangers he may face.""

After De Blasio threw the NYPD under the bus, if I were Dante, I would now be worried more about the danger of being De Blasio's son than my skin color." – Posted by Djones121, WashingtonPost.com

Jokes and snide remarks about the birth names of black children constitute a category unto itself. While the names may often have African or other ethnic origins, many of the unique names bestowed by black parents make it easy for readers to voice their contempt or have a laugh at the expense of others.

One would think that a black child's name was the cause of the trouble that commenter "texasrednek" is speaking about below. The New York Daily News published an article, "Mother's never gonna let go of her miracle baby Zaniyah, infant who dangled from fiery Bronx apt," on Feb. 19, 2010. It was about the bravery of a mother and cousin who saved a baby in an apartment fire. The commenter threw in everything but the kitchen sink of racism:

"these people always seem to find themselves in the soup it seems. If it isnt this woman who give her child some Zulu name its sean bell. Its not an accident that the penile system is filled with them. These people have enough handicaps coming into the world without having some jungle fever name like Zanaya. Whats wrong with a good christian name like, john, david, anthony etc. When the kid grows up and submits resumes using Zanaya, Shanika, Jamaal etc. he better hope he makes it to the NBA or hes gonna have a hard time being taken seriously as he looks for a job" – Posted by texasrednek, NYDailynews.com

I suspect that "texasrednek" was a visitor from the Aryan hate forums, and a lot of his information was incorrect. The baby's name, Zaniyah, is not a traditional Zulu or African name. It "sounds black" but is otherwise invented, according to "ohbabynames.com." The use of the term "jungle fever" is misleading. It actually refers to a nonblack person who is sexually attracted to black people. The director Spike Lee used it as the title for his 1991 film.

Why the commenter threw in Sean Bell's name is a mystery, as its origins are Irish and British. However, he does make a valid point about how African-American names are often used to weed out black employment candidates, but giving a child a traditionally white name still does not guarantee they won't be stereotyped for something else — such as their style of hair or the way they speak.

Jenée Desmond-Harris tackled a unique request on May 16, 2013, in "Race Matters," a question and answer column she writes for "The Root." A woman named "Laquita" was tired of being marginalized for her name and wanted to change it.

"I'm a young black woman with what you would call a 'ghetto' name," she wrote. "I'd have no problem with my name if it weren't for my *entire* life, white people have made fun of me."

The term "ghetto" generally applies to "an area of a city lived in by a minority group, especially a rundown and densely populated area lived in by a group that experiences discrimination," according to the Encarta dictionary. However, the word has come to be most identified with poor black people. Certain names, like this woman's, are considered to be "ghetto," rather than just unique or creative.

The young woman from Desmond-Harris' column was most concerned about having to tell her family, particularly her mother, about the apparent "curse" her mother had placed on her by giving her this name. "Do you think it's the right choice, or am I 'giving up'?" the woman asked.

Desmond-Harris responded in part: "the only thing wrong with 'Laquita,' is that in the minds of those who are so put off by it, it is associated with lower economic status. My view is that the disdain isn't really for the three innocent little syllables but rather, for the type of black person who they imagine would choose to put them together."

So-called "black-sounding" names cause plenty of judgment and discrimination for African-American job seekers, according to a 2003 study from the National Bureau of Economic Research. That study was "Are Emily and Greg More Employable Than Lakisha and Jamal? A Field Experiment on Labor Market Discrimination," a working paper by Marianne Bertrand and Sendhil Mullainathan. It revealed significant discrimination based on names associated with African-Americans. The authors sent resumes in response to job ads in Chicago and Boston newspapers to see how many callbacks each resume would receive for job interviews. On half the resumes, the researchers put white-sounding names like Emily Walsh or Greg Jones. On the other half, they used the "black" names like Lakisha and Jamal.

Nearly 5,000 resumes were sent to more than 1,300 postings for jobs in positions from retail and administrative support to cashier and sales management.

The authors found that white names received 50 percent more callbacks for interviews. Applicants with white-sounding names had to send at least 10 resumes to get one callback, while "black" applicants had to send on average 15. The authors wrote in part, "This 50 percent callback rate is statistically very significant. Based on our estimates, a white-sounding name yields as many callbacks as an additional eight years of experience. Since applicants' names are randomly assigned, this gap can only be attributed to the name manipulation."

Remember the Daily News reader in Chapter 4 who wrote, "How you gonna believe a 14 year old named "Tyasia"!" in response to a story about a teacher accused of using a racial slur during class. As if the responses about the mother whose father had kidnapped her daughter were not racist enough, commenter "NewNicknyc" added this "gem:"

> "Child services should remove the daughter from her custody for child cruelty for naming her Shamiece! Shamiece?!?!? OMG. . . she's going to have a hard childhood! Maybe we should change the mother's name to A S S!!."

In 2009, an unmarried black couple from upstate New York was in a tragic car accident that claimed the life of their 7-year-old son. Their decision to wed at their son's funeral landed their story in the "weird but true" category on parentdish.com, a news and advice website for parents, and drew coverage on CNN.

According to the parents, Amilcar Hill and Rahwa Ghirmatzion, it was their deceased son's wish that they marry. The minister who performed both the funeral and the wedding said that the act "honored" the spirit of the young boy. Comments on the parentdish.com website were far from kind. A number of readers dismissed the act as a publicity stunt and an attempt to make the parents feel better. The critics brutally chastised them because they had not married before.

> "As sad as this situation is, it is another example of the problems in the minority community. Its called the "free breeders." The child had no legal parent as it was. As they say, to little to late." – Posted by Ptango, parentdish.aol.com

Pregnancy before marriage when the parents are white and famous seems to be acceptable and even celebrated. Singer Jessica Simpson had her first child while she was still engaged to her fiancé, an ex-NFL player. While pregnant with her second child out of wedlock, she told Us Weekly magazine in the Jan. 16, 2008, article "Jessica Simpson Talks Second Pregnancy: Eric Johnson 'Keeps Knocking Me Up" that she was ready to get married as soon as the child was born. Perhaps when the woman is already financially secure, there is no rush to seal the deal.

Simpson, who has a reputation for less-than-brilliant comments, told Jay Leno of "The Tonight Show" that she had two wedding dates picked, but that her pregnancies were delaying the wedding. Her solution to meeting her next wedding date, she said, is "just keep my legs crossed."

Reader comments about her remarks on usmagazine.com mostly praised her for being "open and honest," though some referred to her as "Hollywood Trash." Simpson married in July 2014.

Truly, a double standard exists in judging the parenting choices of white celebrities and black families.

"For decades, or longer, the black family has been criticized and seen as 'the problem' rather than looking at the whole social structure and all of the different forces that the black families are subjected to," said Williams, the clinical psychologist in Louisville, Kentucky, interviewed for this book in 2014.

She is the director of the Center for Mental Health Disparities, assistant professor in the Department of Psychological and Brain Sciences at the University of Louisville, and the clinical director of the Behavioral Wellness Counseling Clinic, also in Louisville.

At the University of Louisville, she studies mental health disparities in ethnic and racial minorities — which, according to her, are defined as any situation where one group is getting better treatment than another group, for whatever reason. One of the other important issues that Williams and her colleagues study is race-based trauma. "The effects of racism and discrimination on ethnic minorities do not have to be a burning cross on your lawn to be traumatized by it. It can be the accumulation of small things over time," she said.

Williams said that reading comments that attack African-Americans could constitute race-based trauma.

"I think under the circumstances — getting the dehumanizing and demeaning onslaught against us, these online attacks, the stereotypes, and the economic realities of institutional racism — I think our families have held up very well," Williams said.

She explained how the extended network of support that black families have plays a role.

"Perhaps the father is not in the home, but maybe some other father in the family is there to help raise kids," she said. "Maybe the father's not in the home, but he is available and present. There are a lot of families that don't look like traditional families in the black community; that's not always a bad thing. Sometimes it's different, and there's no need to attach a value judgment to it."

CHAPTER 8

Please Report Offensive Posts!!!!

"In my experience most.blacks don't believe they are capable of racism. They are protesting about cops killing black lives yet ignore the astonishingly disproportionate number of blacks killed by blacks. Statitstics, facts they are of no concern. Make up any story if it fis the narrative. I think the black community has a bit of house cleaning to do before they blame all their problems on the police, government and white privelidge. They can start by being truthful about just who is killing young black men." – Posted by Bernard Curtin, the dailydot.com, July 11, 2014

IN THE EARLY 1990S, THE "information superhighway" became the almost instantaneous connection among millions of people exchanging information from anywhere in the world. The concept of allowing people to comment on stories evolved from the Bulletin Board System, or BBS, which was accessed by a telephone line, as a way to have short conversations via email, discussion boards, online forums, message boards, and chat rooms.

The strategy for websites was to allow readers to write their thoughts in response to content from personal weblogs and news websites in the hopes of generating insightful and engaging dialogue. It did not quite turn out that way. The conversations quickly became at best banal and at worst vicious and decidedly lowbrow. When the conversation turns to race, venomous outpourings of bigotry and hatred dominate the online forums for commentary.

I commend news organizations that spend long hours creating ways to stop the hateful vitriol that appears on their websites. Next to shutting down comment options, the moderation of them has become somewhat of a solution to an embarrassing and controversial problem.

They say that comment moderation, particularly for anonymous posters, is the only way to allow reader interaction peaceably. Because of new rules that force people to be more accountable, such as having them sign on to websites using their Facebook accounts and other identifiers, moderation has been somewhat successful.

The goal of news organization websites was mainly to try to prevent readers — and more importantly, advertisers — from thinking that they tolerated racist opinions on their comment threads, simply by allowing them to be posted. The drawback to the use of both human and technological moderation of racist comments on websites is that it is helping to construct a false illusion that the racism in comment sections is waning.

While it may sometimes appear that there is less racism in the forums, it is only because some comments are being vetted and removed. That does not stop people from rewriting the spiels to make them more acceptable, while still espousing the same racist views, and reposting them to the same site or any other website that would allow them.

In recent years, efforts to sanitize the comments have created several new job titles, from "comment moderator" to "community manager." These are often freelance positions. According to "Comment Moderation, the Dirtiest Job on the Internet," published in Bloomberg Businessweek magazine on Dec. 1, 2011, the need for controlling responses has even allowed for the development of companies such as ICUC Moderation, an organization in London and Canada, that hired 200 moderators globally. It earned $10 million revenue in 2010.

Emoderation, a community management firm also based in London, earned $7 million in revenue since it began in 2002. The firm provides services to MTV, the Economist, and ESPN — charging $4,000 to $50,000 per month.

Both companies sterilize comments on websites and social media engines such as Facebook and Twitter for Chevron, Starbucks, and the Boston Globe.

Emoderation, which now has offices in New York, Los Angeles, and Miami, employs about 350 people. Wendy Christie, its chief production officer in London, said that comment moderation has been available since the 1990s, in the early days of online forums and communities. "The service has boomed since the emergence of social media," she said.

Services include the removal of comments that are offensive, abusive, illegal, obscene, or against the terms of the website to which they are posted. Christie said this protects the hosting organizations from being associated with inappropriate content.

"It also protects the site user from being exposed to content that might be upsetting or illegal," she said.

Other services Emoderation provides to its clients include community management, which Christie said consists of the "building, growing, and guidance" of an online community of people. A community manager encourages people to engage and participate.

"They are the connection point between an organization and members of the community," she said. "They answer questions, help members navigate the site, and post comments on behalf of the organization running the community. Done well, it helps develop a positive relationship between a company and its customers or followers."

There is, however, much more to comment moderation than just yanking offensive comments from websites. First, Christie said, the company provides training for moderators, who must have previous experience, through what she termed project group managers and production teams.

Employees are also "police checked" and trained through another company called Moderation Gateway, which Christie said is the first of its kind. Employees earn a "moderation foundation training certificate" and a place on its "register of trained moderators." The company provides clients with a database of certified moderators.

Although Emoderation would not say whether any of its clients are news organizations, many of their moderators say that the future of online commenting will rely heavily on human content moderators.

Julie Gallagher, its Scotland moderator, said comments must be consistently moderated. "People frequently object to being 'policed' online as it goes against the notion of freedom of speech," she said. "However, there is a fine line between freedom of speech and allowing antagonistic/offensive behavior that would not be acceptable in the real world."

Based on how racist comments have thrived over the last ten years, it is somewhat comforting to know some comments will never see the light of day online, thanks to comment moderation. Yet it seems that for every comment that moderators screen out, ten more will appear on a website that has no qualms about its reader content.

Paul Greenberg, the Tulane media-studies professor, told me that he does not understand the concept of comment moderation. He said that it was "subjective." "It depends on one single individual human being, and it's always one person at a news organization who is moderating the comments. So how do we decide that that person has the capability to do that, and why is his or her opinion on what is acceptable any more acceptable than my opinion?" he asked.

"If you are going to have online communication, it is strictly democratic and that's what a lot of people don't understand that are complaining about online comments," Greenberg told me. "You're going to hear thoughts that bother you. You're going to hear thought processes that bother you. So what? What bothers you doesn't necessarily bother me and vice versa."

Greenberg adamantly opposes comment moderation in any form.

"I don't think that comments should be moderated ever under any circumstances, and I'm proud of my opinion because, if we are going to be a culture that believes in freedom of expression, freedom is not a relative term. Freedom is a finite term. It means free. So those people who object to voices online that are saying things that they find offensive or objectionable do not believe in freedom."

Sarah Hawk, a community manager based in New Zealand who also works for Emoderation, told me that a moderator's decision about offensive comments regarding specific races of people depends on a range of things from agreed-upon guidelines and terms of service to platform capabilities.

"In a modern forum environment, you rely on proactive moderation to a degree, [such as] 'blacklists,' and empower the community to decide (and communicate back) what is appropriate and what is not, using flagging tools," she said.

Older platforms, such as vBulletin, use those flags to alert moderators. Modern platforms such as Discourse automatically hide posts using predefined algorithms.

"A healthy community will employ a team of moderators who are able to use their discretion when it comes to what is appropriate, and in a borderline situation it should be talked through," Hawk said.

Moderation can be tricky, said Suvi Manneh, a moderator and production manager for Emoderation who lives in Gambia, West Africa.

"People are very clever about the way they conceal insults and offending language," Manneh said. "Symbols and numbers are used in place of letters so filters don't catch them, hence the importance of human moderation, and new slang terms come up all the time."

There are, however, some complications in the comment moderation world. "Offensive words can be replaced with the equivalent in another language and so on," Manneh said. "What is offensive varies from country to country and region to region. The term 'colored' to describe a nonwhite person would not be acceptable in the U.K. or the U.S., but is a standard everyday term in South Africa, used by all ethnicities."

Moderating comments may truly be the "dirtiest" job on the Internet. Attention is now being focused on the psychological impact on those who must decide to allow or delete offensive comments. In 2012, Adweek magazine addressed moderators' concerns in the article "Everything in Moderation," published online on June 18, 2013. Justin Isaf, a Huffington Post community manager, told Adweek that people don't understand that there is a huge psychological factor to the job.

"Moderators deal with some horrible stuff and genuinely difficult things every day, and at other sites they are often under-cared-for in terms of their own mental health," he said.

BuzzFeed community moderator Ryan Broderick told Adweek that he interacted with the social news site's "regulars" to keep them from causing too much trouble, but that tensions inevitably abound. "The Trayvon Martin period was a rough couple of weeks," he said, referring to the fatal shooting of a black Florida teenager by an off-duty neighborhood watch participant.

BuzzFeed's "Top Commenter" Joseph Flowers apparently did not appreciate that the president spoke out about the Trayvon Martin case in July 2013. Obama said in part that Martin could have been his son, and that he himself could have been the shooting victim 35 years ago. On its website, BuzzFeed posted the full transcript of the president's remarks.

In his Facebook-registered comment, Flowers wrote:

"If blacks did not rape murder and rob whites EVERYDAY throughout this nation than maybe the whites would not be racist. However since the racist blacks DO rape rob and murder whites EVERDAY and whites do not mess with blacks. The true racists are known. They are not white!!!!!" – Posted by Joseph Flowers, Buzzfeed.com

Many people apparently think freedom of expression gives them license to say things that they instinctively know at the very least are impolite. The satisfaction people feel when they receive affirmative responses to their crippling words enables them to continue.

"It is quite astounding how many 'keyboard warriors' there are out there," said Jen O'Driscoll, an Emoderation moderator based in Australia. "Give people a sense of anonymity and some of them turn hurtful, aggressive, opinionated, and just downright nasty. It's a chilling thought that these folks are more than likely going about their day-to-day activities without their family or colleagues having a clue of what hateful views or aggression they suppress."

The problem of racism online has become such an embarrassment that news editors and organizations are now more openly distancing themselves from racism, whether in comments or in views stated by their own writers outside of their employment. On Oct. 30, 2014, the Charleston Daily Mail in West Virginia fired columnist Don Surber over a posting on his personal blog about African-American shooting victim Michael Brown:

> "This summer I had an epiphany as I watched packs of racists riot in Ferguson, Missouri, in support of a gigantic thug who was higher than a kite when he attacked Ferguson Police Department Officer Darren Wilson, who unfortunately had to put this animal down."

The paper's editor, Brad McElhinny, said: "It's his own blog, but still, he's known as a Daily Mail editorial columnist and many readers seemed to perceive the views stated to reflect on the Daily Mail's editorial policy."

Surber had to know that he would get into trouble for his views. But as O'Driscoll said, people may have an online persona to uphold, possibly for entertainment, out of boredom, or for plain shock value. Many people, she said, may be chronically shy or victims of bullying and use their keyboards as a way to "get back" at the world for hardships they may have had to endure.

In recent years, some news organizations and bloggers also have begun making brave and controversial decisions to do away with comments. On Sept. 24, 2013, popularscience.com said it would shut down comments in response to most news stories, saying that Internet trolls were ruining the online experience of learning about science and that comments caused distractions for readers.

Suzanne LaBarre, the Popular Science online content director, explained the decision.

"Comments can be bad for science," she said. "We are as committed to fostering lively, intellectual debate as we are to spreading the word of science far and wide. The problem is when trolls and spambots overwhelm the former, diminishing our ability to do the latter."

LaBarre said that the magazine would eventually "on occasion" allow comments to stories that "lend themselves to vigorous and intelligent discussion." She said readers could voice their opinions on social media platforms such as Twitter and Google+.

On April 12, 2014, Chicago Sun-Times managing editor Craig Newman announced that the paper would temporarily eliminate story commenting on its website. He explained the decision in "Sick of Internet Comments? Us, Too — here's what we're doing about it," a letter to readers of the Sun-Times.

Newman said in part: "The world of Internet commenting offers a marvelous opportunity for discussion and the exchange of ideas. But as anyone who has ever ventured into a comment thread can attest, these forums too often turn into a morass of negativity, racism, hate speech, and general trollish behaviors that detract from the content. In fact, the general tone and demeanor is one of the chief criticisms we hear in regard to the usability and quality of our websites and articles. Not only have we heard your criticisms, but we often find ourselves as frustrated as our readers are with the tone and quality of commentary on our pages."

Other news organizations are also deleting comments or significantly cutting back on the amount of commenting they allow on their sites. Although it made no big announcement, CNN disabled comments to most stories on its website in August 2014, about the time of the demonstrations in Ferguson, Missouri, over the killing of Michael Brown by a policeman. Readers were not very happy and posted their disgust in other forums such as "godlikeproductions.com," where "Dr Drew" wrote, "Disable any comments of logic by whites especially black on white crime."

In November 2014, Reuters.com ended user comments to news stories. An editor's note headlined "Reader comments in the age of social media," published Nov. 7, 2014, read in part:

"During the past few years, much has changed about how readers interact with news. They find coverage in diverse places and in new ways. They watch video, use graphics and calculators and relate to content far differently than in the past. Considering these dynamics, Reuters.com is ending user comments on news stories. Much of the well-informed and articulate discussion around news, as well as criticism or praise for stories, has moved to social media and online forums. Those communities offer vibrant conversation and, importantly, are self-policed by participants to keep on the fringes those who would abuse the privilege of commenting."

A couple of weeks later, the tech blog Re/code announced that it was deleting its comments section. Re/code co-executive editor Kara Swisher said, "We thought about this decision long and hard, since we do value reader opinion. But we concluded that, as social media has continued its robust growth, the bulk of discussion of our stories is increasingly taking place there, making onsite comments less and less used and less and less useful."

Re/code said it based its decision on Internet trolls and "low quality" conversations in forums.

In other countries, publishers are also dealing with the cesspool of online comments.

At the Toronto Star in Canada, Kathy English, public editor and columnist, suggested that changes to the comment policies were under discussion in a piece published Nov. 14, 2014.

In the column "The incivility of comments: How can the Star reconcile the stew of conflicting views about online commenting?" English said she had been listening to constant complaints about the Star's commenting policies and practices for six years.

She wrote: "I don't think any news organization has figured out an optimal online commenting system that engages readers and encourages civil debates about issues that matter. This is a fraught issue the world over. Judging by the never-ending feedback I receive, it seems no one is happy with online commenting at the Star despite this news organization's best efforts to encourage 'respectful discussion.'"

Overall, English said in her column, some readers wanted real names on comments similar to the letters to the editor pages, while others wanted "wide open" commenting. She said that faction of readers would get "incensed" when the Star did not publish their comments because they did not meet the Star's "community code of conduct."

In response to the question English posed in the subhead line about reconciling conflicting views, she wrote, "I don't have all the answers, but I can tell you that the newsroom is considering the future of online comments."

She said that the newspaper had held many meetings about comments and seemed to be moving toward placing comments on separate pages online, apart from the Star's stories.

"Comments would then be just a click away, perhaps satisfying both those who want to read and engage with comments and those who wish to avoid them," English wrote. "Some other news organizations, notably the New York Times, operate online comments this way."

In the United Kingdom, online comments for the Telegraph and the Guardian are either premoderated or turned off on certain stories. For example, when Margaret Thatcher, Britain's first female prime minister, died on April 9, 2013, the Telegraph shut down comments to any story about her appearing on its site because of "abusive" remarks.

Tony Gallagher, the paper's editor, tweeted his decision: "We have closed comments on every #Thatcher story today — even our address to email is filled with abuse. Many of the people blocked from comments on our #ThatcherCoverage appear to have clogged up my timeline with their foul abuse."

In "Why we sometimes turn comments off," published in the Guardian on May 24, 2012, Gill Phillips, the Guardian's director of editorial legal services, explained that the decision to open or close comments on a story is based on legality. The story was in response to the "Leveson inquiry," a series of public hearings about the culture practices and ethics of the

British press after the highly controversial News International phone hacking scandal.

Phillips wrote in part: "As publishers we are legally responsible for all the output that we produce whether it be news stories, comment above or below the line, and our tweets, etc. This applies equally to matters of contempt as it does to matters of defamation. ... We have to be particularly cautious about tweets and about 'below the line' discussions of matters which are not premoderated and where we cannot expect members of the public to know the subtleties of the law of contempt."

The Guardian story also said that not enabling comments or premoderating were rare occurrences and usually involved topics of a sensitive nature.

A thread might be premoderated, Phillips said, "if the article is a very personal account and we want to avoid abusive and hurtful comments." In addition, the article said that threads might be shut down if the subject was likely to create a hostile or negative discussion and if moderators "feel that the conversation has gone past the point of civility and will not recover."

After seeing how racist comments blanketed its website in 2008, CBS News eventually stopped allowing comments to any story that was about Barack Obama during his first presidential race.

According to Adweek magazine, the makers of Cheerios cereal shut down the comments section of a video of a biracial family depicted in a commercial because it attracted too many racist references to "Nazis" and "racial genocide."

The controversial link-sharing site Reddit was inundated in November 2011 after a thread that encouraged readers to post "extremely controversial things that they honestly believed" presented a shameful view of what our world has come to. A variety of racist and misogynistic responses was posted, including those bemoaning poor white trash as having too many children and no source of income, demeaning women's studies and race studies as a waste of a college major, and ranting about affirmative action promotions.

The bottom line is that society is not benefiting from online reader commentary. No matter what organizations have done or will attempt to do to keep readers on track with positive discourse, short-term solutions do not work. Too many opportunities remain available for people to make negative comments, and merely shutting down the options for certain stories or blocking suspicious users misses the point.

It is easy to fathom why publications want to tolerate comments. They do it mainly to generate page views on their websites, which can increase their revenue by attracting advertisers. Publishing comments gives bigots too large a platform, and creates a space for cyberbullying that encourages incivility and disrespect. How many more subjects of stories have to become victims in online verbal wars, attacked by people they do not know whose only goal is to vent their racism? As if "regular" bullying of school-age children wasn't bad enough, they now have to deal with being cyberbullied by their mean peers. How many young people will feel that their only option is to commit suicide because of the paralyzing effects of online bullying by comments? How many adults would admit to becoming psychologically affected by reading racist remarks and then attempting to defend an entire race against them?

Online comments have become an emotional drug that readers are using to get a quick "high" on racism and hatred.

On our own, we are powerless to stop this. Our humanity will remain in jeopardy as long as the media permits these types of unfiltered comments. The best way to eliminate the problem is to abolish the option to write online comments now and forever.

Wendi Thomas, the former columnist for the Commercial Appeal in Memphis, said her experiences with reader feedback have convinced her that the solution is to remove comments for good. Consider this response to her March 7, 2014, piece "Memphis to sell Forrest Park marker if Confederate group won't reclaim it":

"I wish we could put Wendi in a midtown storage shed. Blacks killing their infants, shooting up malls, murdering, robbing and raping all over town and she rehashes something that was long over with. I wish Wendi would just be honest, she will never be happy until white people are slaves. Many black people feel this way, wake up white people. Stop apologizing for things you didn't do. Stop feeling sorry for these people who wouldn't spit on you if you were on fire, although they would probably steal your wallet. Nothing I said here was any more inflammatory or racist than Wendi's article above, but I bet this disappears before the night is over." – Posted by jonben29#736954, Commercialappeal.com

The story was about a stone tribute marker for Confederate general Nathan Bedford Forrest, the first known Ku Klux Klan grand wizard, which was owned by the Sons of Confederate Veterans. The relic had been removed by the Memphis City Council from a park that also bore his name.

Thomas reported that it had been sitting in a midtown storage shed since January 2013 and was possibly going to be auctioned off if no one claimed it.

The reader did not appreciate her dredging up the embarrassing Klan history and decided instead to shift the focus to their perceptions of black people that were irrelevant to the story.

"Turn off the comments," Thomas said.

It would never be that easy, though. She says the Commercial Appeal has a strict policy against turning off comments. Ever.

"I think that's foolish, but they never turn them off," she said. "After the first five negative comments, what's the point? You're subjecting your staff to a level of abuse that is unprecedented."

On Jan. 20, 2015, the Commercial Appeal published the article "Explaining why comments suddenly disappear," about the paper's moderation guidelines and the management's enforcement of those policies. Gary Robinson, the paper's digital managing editor, wrote: "We are often accused of being 'poof happy,' that we remove comments left and right every day. Just for a little context, our moderation program allows us to look at certain metrics. As I write this, we have removed 2.5 percent (105) of the past 4,204 comments so we do it sparingly. And we never do it because of a philosophical or political disagreement with the comment."

At the end of the article, he provided a list of things that the Commercial Appeal did not want in their comments. They included among others, "name calling" that included calling people racists, bigots, or trolls and "stereotyping," the lumping in a group by race, ethnicity, neighborhood, or sports team affiliation.

On March 27, 2015, the Commercial Appeal officially announced that it and other publications then owned by the E.W. Scripps Co. would start requiring that readers comment through Facebook as of Monday, March 30, 2015. The reason, the Appeal said, was that a third-party moderation program provider had gone out of business. Of the change, the Appeal staff wrote, "Facebook is the most widely used platform for sharing and conversation. We also thought that it would be good to treat online comments in a similar fashion as we do other forms of reader comments, such as Letters to the Editor."

Like many other online news organizations, the Commercial Appeal is using Facebook, presumably to hold people accountable for their comments. In order to belong to Facebook, people are supposed to use their real names, and Facebook monitors compliance. According to the Facebook.com help center, "Facebook is a community where people use their authentic identities. We require people to provide the name they use in real life."

Gallagher, the Emoderation moderator based in Scotland, said that a successful comments section or forum should be one that generates opinion, interest, or useful information for the community for which it was designed.

"This can sometimes include heated debates and extreme opinions," she said. "Along with freedom of speech comes the freedom to be offended and express that offense."

Steve Freeman, the Anti-Defamation League associate director in New York, says that freedom of speech actually does not protect people who post racist comments.

"There are some sites that say look, anything goes. We're not going to impose any guidelines or any terms of service or anything," he said. "In that case, they're basically setting up what amounts to an open forum for free speech, but the vast majority of major Internet platforms, certainly all the major social media platforms, have standards, and they're not governed by the First Amendment because they are not government."

However, when anyone checks off "yes" to the terms of service of a website, and then writes something that they agreed that they would not, the website can take it down. In that moment, they will assume that their freedom of speech and expression has been violated, when actually they agreed not to do what they did.

Freeman thinks the focus on combating online offenders will be finding the most "effective means" of counter-speech. One example he cited was the stream of nasty things people said on Twitter about Rima Fakih, the first Muslim Miss USA, who was crowned in 2010.

"That was overwhelmed by a barrage of people saying that she was great and that 'We're thrilled' and 'You're an idiot' and so forth," Freeman said. "It was to the point where the end of the story was a really positive one because the marketplace worked. That can be lots and lots of people or it can be just one person with a huge following who says something positive about the first gay basketball player, who has half a million followers."

Mark Potok at Southern Poverty Law Center thinks that shutting comments off, as I would like, isn't a good solution. He said that more speech is better than less speech, but also understands that the comments can be extremely hurtful. "At the end of the day, it's probably better to shine a light on what people are really feeling than to pretend that it isn't so," he said. "You want to deal with racism in society and understand what's actually there. It's not a theoretical exercise, so I think it's better to face the reality and deal with that, [rather] than live in some Pollyanna world where we all love each other and nobody ever says anything unpleasant."

Days, the Philadelphia Daily News editor, is for keeping comments, but thinks they could be monitored better.

"I think we have to figure out a way to pay for people to engage with commenters," he said. "That doesn't mean we're pulling out everything that we don't like, but I think there needs to be some kind of discussion with the entity that is producing the content and the commentary."

"That doesn't mean that we're like, 'Shame, shame on you,' but maybe forcing people to think a little bit about what they're putting up there" would help, he said.

That conversation, he thinks, might go something like this:

Poster: "All these people need to be in jail. All these people they deserve to be in jail.

Editor: "Why do you think that? How did you get to that point? What's driving your conversation to that?"

Doing this, Days said, would engage people who actually have something to say and those who want to have a dialogue about controversial issues.

"I think that's what we should be fostering, not the crazies. They hate Obama. They hate diversity. They hate immigration," he said. "They want the world the way it was in 1953, and it's not going to be that way," he said.

William Turner, a lecturer at the University of California Berkeley, says that shutting off comments is purely an editorial decision.

"For reasons that I don't fully understand, encouraging reader comments, like encouraging radio call-ins, seems to be good for business," he said.

The Denver Post, part of Digital First Media, uses the moderation platform Disqus, while other papers in the chain make people register to comment through a Facebook plug-in. Even with that, comments still are moderated by staffers, Post editor Moore said.

"Everybody just pitches in, different people on the digital side. ... We know what stories to sort of look at," he said. "We know if we got a story about the Dream Act and three girls desperately want to go to college and who are valedictorians at their schools, we know we are going to get a lot of blowback from that."

Although comment moderation has helped to block many offensive anonymous responses, it has not made enough of an impact for society to breathe a collective sigh of relief. If websites insist on allowing racist, homophobic, xenophobic, sexist, and other destructive comments, those companies should be fined for allowing their readers the "privilege" of spewing their vitriol for the world to see and using their websites as a platform to do it.

Since it is impossible for websites and humans to be self-policing when it comes to comments, it should all come down to the bottom line. Just as Chuck D says in his foreword for this book, if ISPs were made responsible for what readers post to the websites of their clients and if a comment-policing organization could impose fines, we would not have as much of a problem with negative comments as we do today.

Such a comment-policing organization could regulate comments for all websites, especially for companies that do not want to shut them off.

An organization such as this could help to rein in bad responses and make companies comply when they receive warnings that could lead up to paying fines for comments that include racism, xenophobia, homophobia, sexism, and all of the negativity that has made reading comments a generally unpleasant experience. This means any negative comment written by a person of *any* race. The comment sections of websites should be a safe haven for readers.

Berkeley's Turner, who is also a freedom of speech lawyer and author of "Figures of Speech: First Amendment Heroes and Villains," Sausalito, California, PoliPointPress, 2011, disagreed with my suggestion for regulating comments.

"I doubt that regulation by some outside agency would work — too slow, clumsy, and uncertain," he said. "What standards would they use? One thing that is crystal clear: Government should not be involved in any way. Involving government implicates the First Amendment ban on censorship. Online publishers can't violate the First Amendment with their terms of use and censorship of comments, as only government can violate the First Amendment."

Granted, deciding to read comments is a *choice*, but like fast-food commercials on television, comments are difficult for some people to ignore. Websites know that. They want you to stay, to keep on reading and adding your own two cents on any topic.

Having an organization that imposes strict fines for websites would certainly make any publication start to question whether comments are valuable to them.

Greenberg, the Tulane professor, told me that I support shutting off the comments because I am of a "certain culture," of a "certain race," and that I'm reading highly offensive things into them. He's not wrong there, and he agrees that I should be offended.

"But where would you draw the line — at Nigerians? Would you draw the line at Canadians? If we offend Canadians, should we then cut those off? If we offend people who live in a South Pacific Island, should we cut that off?" he asked me. "Where are we going to cut this off? Because if we cut off every racial comment stream that occurs, then we cut off all comment streams and there are no online comments."

The future of commenting depends on just how much news organizations and others are going to want to continue dealing with repercussions. Both journalists and moderators seem to agree that comment moderation and fighting back are going to be the strongest ways to control online commenting. That may well be, but it costs money to hire moderators, and with competition from the Internet and the economic realities of recent years that have forced the news industry to resort to massive layoffs and buyout options, would it even be cost effective? For newsrooms with smaller staffs, is it fair to have editors and journalists serving double duty, moderating comments when they are already at the brink of exhaustion from their regular duties? What if people just get so tired of trying to fight the trolls that they stop reading a particular website altogether?

Every day as I read racist comments for this book, I thought about my mental health. The experience of swimming in such a volatile pool of hatred has probably harmed me in ways that I have not yet realized. Recall that Louisville psychologist Williams told me that the experience of reading racist comments *is* race-based trauma. Although I've not experienced a cross burning on my lawn, the accumulation of small hurts over time constitutes trauma. She said reading so many negative things about something that is so central to me, as in the plight of African-Americans, tends to take a toll.

Negative reader comments present African-Americans to the public as a wayward race of people who lack the most basic of morals or self-control and who have little to offer in any profession. As we have seen in Chapter Two, "Fear of a Black President," from the scores of hysterically racist comments we do not live in a post-racial society and probably never will.

Wade, the clinical psychologist in San Francisco, told me that education is the key to counteracting the negativity in comments. She said that people who write the hate-filled comments suffer from tremendous ignorance and don't know anything about the world.

"They need exposure, education and boundaries and checks in place," she said.

More important, she said, African-Americans should be conscious of racist comments and should understand that we have the right to be angry and sad about them. She suggested an affirmation to counter the effects: "At the end of the day, they are not going to take my power. I'm not giving it to them."

I can certainly agree with her and take her advice, but I have my doubts about whether many of the people writing the racist screeds, who are likely already set in their ways, are open to change.

The problem of racist comments about news stories may never be solved. I am, however, pleased that with this book I have added my voice of concern about this ugly aspect of Internet history. Together with industry leaders and concerned Internet users, I hope we may rise above this and other affronts on the psyche of African-American people, so that we can continue to enrich our legacy and news sites can flourish in an atmosphere of civility and respect for all users.

Index

2008 presidential race, 36–43
2012 presidential race, 55–56

Adams, Eric L., 21, 25, 50, 85
Adrine, Ronald, 126–27
alcohol billboards targeting
    African-Americans, 31
Allen, Harry, 68–69
anonymity of Internet, 8–9, 14–15,
    19, 163. *See also:* court orders
    unmasking anonymity
Anthony, Robert S., 2, 37
Anti-Defamation League, 10–12,
    171–72
anti-SLAPP law, 15
Ardia, David, 15
athletes, black, 141–42

Bailey, Robert, 151
Balfour, Michele Davis, 83
Balfour, William, 71, 83
Baltimore, 98, 123–24
Bartletteer, 16, 17

Beard, Jesse Ray, 151
"Beating the Odds: Raising
    Academically Successful
    African American Males," 109
"Beer Summit," 52–53
Bell, Mychal, 149–50
Bell, Nicole Paultre, 58–59
Bell, Sean, killing of, 21, 57–59,
    152–53
Berkeley, Terry, 88–89
Bernhard, Sandra, 138
Bertrand, Marianne, 154
Bilal, Rochelle, 20
Bishop, Amanda, 88, 90
black children, 6, 13, 81–83, 86, 103,
    107, 110, 143–57
    education, 12–13, 102–113
    "ghetto" children, 79, 87, 103,
    144–45
    welfare, 86–87
black fraternities, 5–6
black journalists, 42, 61
black marriage, myths about, 76–79

black men
  animal instinct, 114–142
  athletes, 141–142
  crime stories, 135, 137–39
  earnings, 77
  Eric Garner case, 120–22, 151
  fatherhood, 79, 81–83, 143
  Freddie Gray case, 123–24
  John Crawford case, 127–29
  Michael Brown case, 118–20, 151, 164
  racial profiling, 13–14, 52–53, 65–66, 130–32
  relations with women, 73–76
  statistics on discrimination, 135–36
  Tamir Rice case, 125–27
  Trayvon Martin case, 60, 114–18, 133, 163
black parenting, 143–57
black professional basketball players, 147
black women
  D.C. sniper's wife, 91
  domestic violence, 84–85
  finding black men, 75–76
  Jennifer Hudson case, 71, 73–74, 83
  Joseph Robinson case, 92–93
  Malia/Sasha dolls, 99–100
  marriage statistics, 77
  Michelle Obama, 41, 96–98, 100–101
  Natavia Lowery case, 73
  overview of hostility toward, 71–101
  Phaedra Parks case, 93–95
  Shanesha Taylor case, 87–91
Blair, Jayson, 45
Bloomberg, Michael, 132
bodegas, New York City, 146
"boy," as derogatory term, 44–45
Braconi, Frank, 136
Broderick, Ryan, 163
Brown vs. Board of Education, 102
Brown, Chris, 85
Brown, Michael, 118–20, 151, 164–65
bulletin board systems, 4–5, 28, 158
Bush, George W., 49
Butler, Bob, 1–2, 11, 118, 125

Carr, Gwen, 122
cartoons
  Colt 45 malt liquor, 31–32
  fist-bumping terrorists, 41
  Obama as Joker, 43
  pet chimp, 47–50
castration, 137
CBS News, 168
Cebull, Richard, 44
Central Park, 151
Charleston Daily Mail, 164
Chavis, Ben, 68
Cheerios ad, 168
Chicago Sun-Times, 165

chimpout.com, 113

chokeholds, 120–122

Christie, Wendy, 160

Chuck D, *xi–xiv*, 106, 174

Church of God in Christ story, 25–26

civil rights lawsuits, 20–21

CNN, 64–65, 119

Coalition to Stop Gun Violence PSA, 116

Cohen, Liskula, 19

comment forums, origin of, 4–5, 158

comment-policing organization, 174

community funding disparities, 81

Congressional Black Caucus, 54

convicts, marginalization of, 91–92

corner stores, New York City, 146

court orders unmasking anonymity, 15, 18–19

Crawford, John, 127–29

crowdfunding, 88, 90

Crowley, James, 51–53

Cumbo, Laurie, 22–24, 81

Curtis, Mary C., 38

cyberbullying, 169

"Cyber Racism: White Supremacy Online and the New Attack on Civil Rights," 35

Daniels, Cora, 146

Daniels, Jessie, 35

Days, Michael, 7, 34, 145, 172–73

D.C. sniper, 91

De Blasio, Bill, 151–52

defamation suits, 15, 18–19

Denver Post, 27, 61–62, 173

Desmond-Harris, Jenée, 76–77, 153–54

Detroit, 31–32, 139–40

discipline of black students, 111

disclaimers, 26–27

Discourse, 162

discrimination
    based on names, 154–55
    Central Park 5, 151
    Jena 6, 149–50
    statistics on, 135–37

discussion guidelines, 26

Disqus, 173

domelights.com, 20–21

domestic violence, 84–85

double standards, 49, 63–65, 85, 96, 125, 143–44, 148, 156

Dougherty, John J., 18

Duncan, Arne, 111

Eady, Kermit, 92

education, equal, 102–113

effects of racist comments
    on health, 30–31
    on journalists, 16, 145
    on moderators, 162–63
    on young people, 33–34
    race-based trauma, 156–57, 176

Emoderation, 159–62
ending comments, 164–68
English, Kathy, 166–67

Facebook, commenting via, 171
Fakih, Rima, 172
Feminist Majority Foundation,
    84–85
Ferguson shooting, 64–65, 118–20,
    164–65
Figueroa, Dahlma Llanos, 110–11
"Figures of Speech: First
    Amendment Heroes and
    Villains," 174
First Amendment rights, 1, 10–11
fist bump, 40–41
flagging comments, 11, 162. *See
    also:* moderating comments
Flowers, Joseph, 163
fratty.net, 5–6, 17
freedom of expression, 1–3, 161,
    163, 171, 174–75
freedom of speech, 1
    vs. freedom of expression, 1–3.
    See also: freedom of expression
Freeman, Steve, 11, 171–72
Fulton, Sybrina, 117–18, 133

Gallagher, Julie, 161, 171
Gallagher, Tony, 167
"Game Change," 37
gang rape stereotype, 138–39, 151
Gardere, Jeff, 149

Garmback, Frank, 126
Garner, Eric, 120–23, 151
Gates Jr., Louis, 51–53
Gates, Bill, 146
"ghetto children," 144–45
ghetto names, 153–54
"Ghettonation: Dispatches from
    America's Culture War," 146
Ghirmatzion, Rahwa, 155
graduation rates of black students,
    112
grammatical errors in comments,
    6–7
grandmothers, young, 79
Gray, Freddie, 123–24
Greenberg, Paul, 10, 161, 175
Greene, David, 18
Griffin Sr., Tarrance, 86
Guardian Civic League, 20
Guardian, 167–68
Gun-control laws, 63–64
guns, toy, 125–30

Halloran, Liz, 54–55
hate crimes, racist speech, 18
hate sites – *See:* racist websites
Hawk, Sarah, 162
health effects of racist comments,
    30–31. *See also:* effects of racist
    comments
hearsay as evidence, 8–9
Herbert, Bob, 52–53
Hill, Amilcar, 155

hip-hop music, 42–43, 67–68, 80
Holder, Eric, 50–51, 126
Holloway, Lynette, 149
Holmes, James Egan, 63, 125
Holmes, Santonio, 141
Hoskins, Nichele, 28
Hrabowski III, Freeman, 109
Hudson, Jennifer, 71, 73–74, 83

ICUC Moderation, 159
intellectual inferiority, 13. *See also:*
    education, equal
Isaf, Justin, 162–63
ISPs, liability, 3–4, 174

James, LeBron, 142
Jena 6 case, 149–51
Jobs, Steve, 146
Johnson, LeeCee, 127
Johnson, Magic, 62
Jones, Jim, 45–46
Journal of Black Higher Education,
    112
"jungle fever," 153

Kappa Sigma fraternity, 6, 17
Kilpatrick, Kwame, 139–40
Klein, Joel I., 108
Klein-Sharpton initiative, 108–9
Ku Klux Klan, 7, 21, 170

LaBarre, Suzanne, 164–65
Lanza, Adam, 148

Lauter, Deborah, 12
Lee, Spike, 153
Léger, Daniella Gibbs, 46–47
Leveson inquiry, 167–68
Loehmann, Timothy, 126
Lohner, Steve, 125
"Long Shadow of Incarceration's
    Stigma," 93
Louis, Errol, 53
Lowery, Natavia, 73

"Malcolm X: A Life of Reinvention,"
    55
Malvo, Lee Boyd, 91
Manneh, Suvi, 162
Marable, Manning, 55
Marks, Bryant, 77
Martin, Tracy, 117–18
Martin, Trayvon, 16, 60, 114–18,
    133–34, 163
Mbeki, Thabo, 139
McElhinny, Brad, 164
Memphis Commercial Appeal, 16,
    25–26, 61, 169–71
Miami Herald website, 26–27
Miller, E. Ethelbert, 29
Mitchell, Mary, 71, 83–84
moderating comments, 11, 26–27,
    159–74
Moore, Gregory L., 7, 27–28, 61–
    62, 173
Mosby, Marilyn, 124
Moynihan, Daniel, 64

Muhammad, John Allen, 91
Muhammad, Mildred, 91
Mullainathan, Sendhil, 154
Murch, Donna, 64

N-word, 37, 44, 62, 103–6
names, black, 150, 152–54
Nathan Bedford Forrest memorial, 170
Nelson, Sophia A., 96–97
New York Civil Liberties Union, 9, 130
Newman, Craig, 165
Nida, Apollo, 93–94
No Child Left Behind Act, 12–13, 107
"Notorious" film, 24, 66–67, 69–70
NYPD
    crime statistics, 65–66
    Eric Garner death, 120–22
    NYPD rant, 21
    rap intelligence unit, 67–68
    stop-and-frisk policy, 130–32

O'Driscoll, Jen, 163
Obama, Barack
    2008 presidential race, 36–43
    2012 presidential race, 55–56
    Antichrist, 47
    CBC address, 54
    comparison to Jim Jones, 45–46
    fatherhood talk, 81–82
    fist bump, 40–41

Gates/Crowley situation, 51–53
    hostility toward, 36–56
    interrupting, 46–47
    lack of focus on race relations, 53–54
    misspelling of name, 45
    pet chimpanzee cartoon, 47–49
Obama, Malia and Sasha, 99–100
Obama, Michelle, 40–41, 96–101
Oher, Michael, 142
"one-upmanship" in comments, 31–33
Ottinger, Richard, 15

Palin, Bristol, 79–80
Palin, Sarah, 79, 138
Pantaleo, Daniel, 121
Parker, Derrick, 67–68
Parks, Phaedra, 93–95
Paterson, David, 29
Philadelphia Daily News, 145
Philadelphia police department, 17–18, 20–21
Phillips, Gill, 167–68
philly.com, 18, 145
police altercations, 57–70
politics and racism, 36–37, 43–44. See also: 2008 presidential race, 2012 presidential race
Popular Science, 164–65
Port, Rosemary, 19
Post, Tim, 13
post-racial society, 2, 38, 55, 98, 176

Potok, Mark, 8, 112–13, 172

Prince, Sabiyha, 37, 87

prison sentences of black men, 135. *See also:* convicts, marginalization of

Pumpkin Fest riot, 64

Purvis, Bryant, 151

"Race Relations on Campus" report, 17

"Race, Riots, and Roller Coasters: The Struggle Over Segregated Recreation in America," 65

race-based trauma, 156–57, 176

racial disparities in welfare, 87

racial profiling, 13–14, 52–53, 65–66, 130–32

racist websites
chimpout.com, 113
domelights.com, 20–21
NYPD rant, 21
stormfront.org, 7, 150
Vanguard News Network, 7
See also: typical racist statements

rap music, 67–68. *See also:* hip-hop music

Re/code, 166

"Real Housewives of Atlanta," 93–95

Reddit, 168

"regular folks" and racism, 7

regulation of Internet speech, 3–4

Reid, Harry, 37

Remnick, David, 41

reparations for slavery, 44–45

Reuters, 165–66

Rice, Tamir, 125–27

Rihanna, 85

Riordan, Carol Ann, 26

Robinson, Gary, 26

Robinson, Joseph, 92–93

Romney, Mitt, 55

Roosevelt, Long Island, 129, 144 school district, 102–3

Rule, Sheila, 91–92

Sacco, Elvira, 104–5

Samuels, Allison, 60–61

"Scared Silent," 91

Scheindlin, Shira, 130, 135

Section 230 of the Communications Decency Act, 3

segregation in public schools, 102

Sharpton, Rev. Al, 32, 38–39, 48–49, 58–59, 108, 120, 132

Shaw, Theo, 151

Shedden, David, 4

Sheen, Charlie, 85

Siegel, Norman, 2, 9–11, 18–19, 55

Simpson, Jessica, 155–56

Sirota, Jeff, 148

"Son of Sam," 129

South Africa, 139

Southern Poverty Law Center, 8, 112, 172

St. Cloud Times website, 13–14
Stein, Linda, 73
Stephens-Davidowitz, Seth, 55–56
Sterling, Donald, 62
Stone, Lisa, 19
stop-and-frisk policy, 130–35
stormfront.org, 7, 150
Strategic Lawsuits Against Public Participation law, 15
Sturgis, Ingrid, 75
Suleman, Nadya, 85
Surber, Don, 164
Swift, Taylor, 96
Swisher, Kara, 166

Taylor, Shanesha, 87–91
teen pregnancy, 79–80
Telegraph, London, 167
Temporary Assistance for Needy Families, 87
Thatcher, Margaret, 167
Thee Rant website, 21–22
Think Outside the Cell Foundation, 92
Thomas, Wendi C., 16–17, 61, 169–70
Title V of the Telecommunications Act of 1996, 3
Toldson, Ivory A., 77
Toronto Star, 166–67
toy guns, 125–30
Trice, Dawn Turner, 42
Turner, William, 173, 174

types of people posting racist comments, 7
typical racist statements, 6, 8, 44

unemployment statistics, 136–37
University of South Carolina fraternities, 5–6, 17

Vanguard News Network, 7
vBulletin, 162
violence, accusations of, 22, 24–25, 114, 133–34

Wade, Brenda, 30–31, 80, 176
Walters, Janice, 3, 31
"war on women" catchphrase, 72
Wasow, Omar, 4–5
welfare, 79, 86–87
white supremacist forums, 7–8. See also: racist websites
Williams, Jumaane, 130
Williams, Monnica, 95, 156–57
Williams, Venus, 61
Wolcott, Victoria W., 65
Woods, Keith, 9, 12, 31, 61
Woods, Tangernika, 86
Wright, James, 5
Wright, Jerome, 25–26

Zimmerman, George, 16, 60, 114–16
Zuleger, Dean, 14–15

About the Author

ANITA M. SAMUELS IS A nationally acclaimed journalist and critic who writes about media, fashion, music, and culture. A frequent contributor to *The New York Daily News*, Samuels began her career on the staff of *The New York Times* style section, where a number of her features about the African-American community earned her an award from the National Association of Black Journalists in 1992. Samuels has been an editor for national publications as *BET Weekend*, *Billboard*, *Heart & Soul*, and *Impact Radio, Records and Retail Weekly*. Her stories have also appeared in *Essence, The Source, Consumer's Digest, Global Rhythm* magazine, *The Asbury Park Press, Upscale, Honey, CODE, Caribbeat, Forum, Child Magazine,* fiercefor-blackwomen.com and diversebusinessnews.com, among others. She was a contributing writer for *Mama's Little Baby: The Black Woman's Guide to Pregnancy, Childbirth and Baby's First Year*. Samuels resides in Brooklyn, New York.

www.ingramcontent.com/pod-product-compliance
Lightning Source LLC
Chambersburg PA
CBHW071147050326
40689CB00011B/2018